BY **MELANIE TAIT**

HOW TO PLOT A HIT IN TWO DAYS

CURRENCY PRESS
The performing arts publisher

CURRENT THEATRE SERIES

First published in 2025
by Currency Press Pty Ltd,
Gadigal Land, Suite 310, 46–56 Kippax Street, Surry Hills, NSW 2010, Australia
enquiries@currency.com.au
www.currency.com.au

in association with Ensemble Theatre

Typeset by Brighton Gray for Currency Press.
Printed by Fineline Print + Copy Services, Revesby.
Cover shows Georgie Parker; photo by Brett Boardman. Cover design by Alphabet Studio.

Currency Press acknowledges the Traditional Owners of the Country on which we live and work. We pay our respects to all Aboriginal and Torres Strait Islander Elders, past and present.

A catalogue record for this book is available from the National Library of Australia

How to Plot a Hit in Two Days is a fictional play imagining the machinations of a hypothetical writers' room. It is not affiliated with the television show *A Country Practice.*

Contents

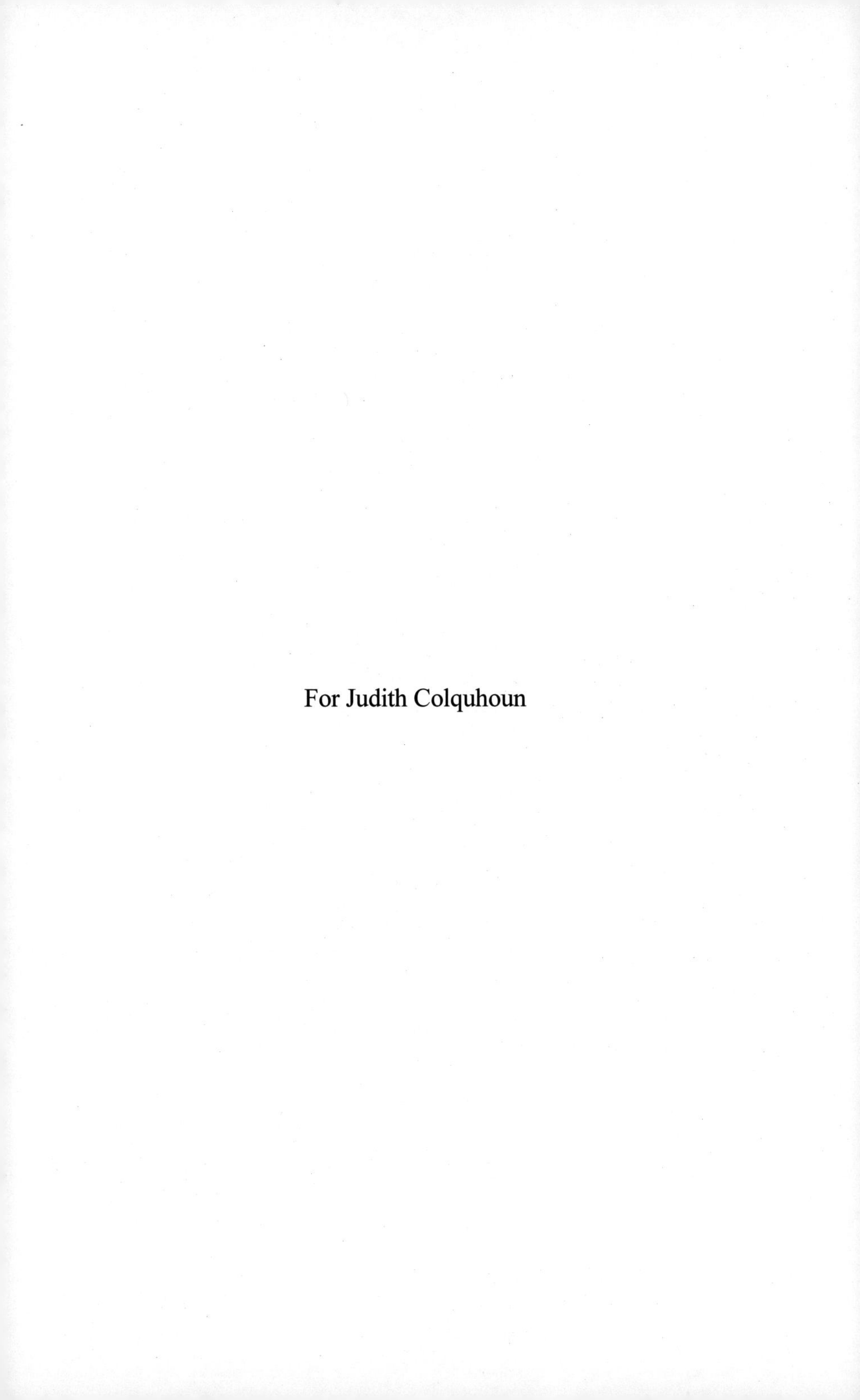

For Judith Colquhoun

How To Plot A Hit In Two Days was first produced by Ensemble Theatre, Cammeraygal Country, Kirribilli, on 29 August 2025 with the following cast:

SHARON	Amy Ingram
DELL	Genevieve Lemon
BERT	Seán O'Shea
JUDY	Georgie Parker
SALLY	Julia Robertson

Director, Lee Lewis
Assistant Director, Tiffany Wong
Set and Costume Designer, Simone Romaniuk
Lighting Designer, Brockman
Composer and Sound Designer, Paul Charlier
Stage Manager, Jen Jackson
Assistant Stage Manager, Sherydan Simson
Costume Supervisor, Renata Beslik

CHARACTERS

BERT, forties

JUDY, forties

SALLY, twenties

SHARON, twenties or forties

DELL

This playtext went to press before the end of rehearsals and may differ from the play as performed.

PART ONE

The A Country Practice Story *Conference Room.*

Enter BERT *(forties).*

He carries a satchel filled with scripts, cassettes etc.

He switches on the lights.

This isn't your average conference room. It's where writers are expected to come up with ideas, so it's comfortable, lived in and welcoming.

There's a table in the middle of the room, it's bare right now.

There's a couch.

A television and video player on wheels. Beta tapes stacked nearby of past episodes.

A sound system with decent speakers. It's mostly used for cassettes.

A tea and coffee station. Kettle and various instant coffees and tea bags.

A bar fridge is stacked with beers, cans of soft drinks, wine and champagne.

On the back wall is a cork board where episodes will be beat out.

There's some butchers paper on a stand.

There are headshots of the 'Main Cast' (Shane Porteous TERENCE, Brian Wenzel FRANK, Lorrae Desmond SHIRLEY, Grant Dodwell SIMON, Penny Cook VICKI, Anne Tenney MOLLY, Shane Withington BRENDAN) and 'Supporting Cast' (Emily Nicol CHLOE, Gordon Piper BOB, Sydney Heylen COOKIE, Joyce Jacobs ESME, Joan Sydney MATRON and Wendy Strehlow JUDY) hung up.

Countless awards and certificates are displayed proudly: Logies etc.

It's not a conference room to be dreaded. It's got a warm and inviting energy. Like BERT.

Before he begins to set up the room, he takes a cassette out of his satchel and puts it into the player. The Overture of The Marriage of Figaro.

He lights a cigarette and begins to set up the room. He goes in and out of the room collecting stuff for the tasks he has. Ciggie never leaves his mouth.

He sets five notepads onto the table. Puts a box of fresh lead pencils into a container. Places five erasers in each spot.

Opens a couple of bags of Minties and Fantales. Pops them into a bowl, places the bowl in the middle of the table.

Brings in two clean ashtrays. Places at either side of the table.

Labels five coffee cups (JUDY, BERT, DELL, SALLY, SHARON) and places them in each spot.

Once the room is prepared, he takes out a notebook and pencil from his satchel, sits on the couch, closes his eyes and waits for inspiration to strike while savouring his cigarette.

Enter JUDY *(forties).*

JUDY: Today's going to be a day and a half.
BERT: Sure is.
JUDY: Here—

Out of her bag comes a carton of B&H ciggies to add to the table of lollies, etc.

Did you read it?
BERT: Of course!
JUDY: What a—
BERT: I've been thinking about it all morning—
JUDY: What is this music?
BERT: Figaro.
JUDY: It's a lot.
BERT: You should see it while you're in town.
JUDY: I'm in Sydney!
I can't be spending two hours watching sweaty old tenors yelling at me—
BERT: A sweaty old tenor can make you so warm inside, Jude.
Don't you want to be warm inside?
JUDY: If I was any warmer inside I'd start to caramelise.
BERT: A serious woman of poetry, who doesn't like opera? Makes no sense.

JUDY: An unserious man of jokes, who loves opera? You're the mystery, Berto.

BERT: I'll get you to an opera one day.
We just haven't found you the right one yet.

JUDY: If you can find one when they're not singing all the time, I'm there.
Oy! She'll be here soon.

BERT: What are we going to do?
Pretend we haven't read it?

JUDY: She'll know we've read it.

BERT: Every word of it is tray-ush.

JUDY: It's a brain fart and Dell's the victim of the after-stink.

BERT: Surely she won't care.

JUDY: She'll care.
She'll make out like she doesn't, but she'll care.
I care.
If I ever see that skuzzy little nothing, I'll throw a red wine in his gouty face.

BERT: Rachel Ward already did.

JUDY: She did?

BERT: In the foyer at the Stables. Penny has a great story about it.

JUDY: I miss all the good stuff living in the country.

BERT: Someone writing on *A Country Practice* needs to live in the country.
What are we going to do?

JUDY: We're going to be good friends.
We're going to be sympathetic, then we'll meet at dawn to action his demise!

BERT: They don't call you TV's greatest killer for nothing.

JUDY: What a shame for Dell my killing skills are only linguistic.

BERT: Surely it's about mindset Jude.
Words are powerful.
I believe in you.
I reckon you could kill for Dell.

JUDY *is unpacking her gear and getting set up for the day's work.*

JUDY: I still get so excited about being here!

BERT: Bonza ratings, eh?

JUDY: There's a bit of an Esme type at home—when we have an ep she likes, she drops in some lemon slice.

This week, lemon slice and lemon cake.

BERT: Maybe Evelyn and I should move to the country.

JUDY: You'd be bored shitless, Berto.

I don't think you'd get quite the same sweaty yelling hit from the Berry Gilbert and Sullivan Society.

BERT: I could finally offer up my Pirate King!

JUDY: You'd be fighting Barry for it!

BERT: How is Barry? And Chloe? And Luke?

JUDY: Nothing much changes down there.

I really shouldn't be here this week. Chloe's sitting the School Certificate.

BERT: I thought the School Certificate didn't matter anymore.

JUDY: Everything matters to Chloe.

BERT: What's that thing they say about apples not falling far from trees?

JUDY: Have we used that as an ep title yet?

BERT: Surely?

JUDY: Not on my watch.

He writes it down.

How are your girls?

BERT: Jo's loving being in the States, away from us—

JUDY: Must be costing you a fortune!

BERT: Evelyn's family own the university or donate to it or however it works with those Americans. Latin words. Alumni. Summa cum laude. Quibus non existentibus.

JUDY: She didn't want to study here?

BERT: 'I'm sorry Dad, Australia is just too small for me.'

JUDY: Does Evelyn get homesick?

BERT: I don't think so.

JUDY: You haven't asked her?

BERT: Do you think I should?

JUDY: Of course I think you should.

BERT: Evelyn's gone and got a job!

JUDY: Good on her!

BERT: With Hoges. In Darwin!

JUDY: Darwin! What a bloody nightmare!

BERT: She's being pretty unbearable about working in 'film'.

JUDY: As opposed to us plebs slumming in in TV?

BERT: Apparently, it's the next *Gallipoli* but instead of Mel Gibson you've got Hoges and a crocodile. Good luck, my darling. I hope my *Country Practice* wage buys you a delicious meal at one of Darwin's many fine dining restaurants.

Enter a furious DELL *with a newspaper in her hand—she holds it like it's on fire ... or is a sacred conch. This is a woman full of the most fabulous sort of drama.*

The three of them look at each other—terrified. Who's going to break the silence? Who's going to speak of this great treachery first!?

DELL: 'Overwrought, overwritten, obvious and odious!'

'Oh look, Eleven Readers of *The Mirror*'s Woeful Theatre Section:

Your critic has taken a moment away from showing young actors his member to demonstrate to you he knows about assonance!'

JUDY: Fooey to that guy.

DELL: No-one ever fooeys that guy. That's the problem.

He's the way he is because the pleasures of the flesh are denied him so completely.

Revolting little man.

BERT: I laughed sixty-seven times, which is a joke rate my old mate Lucille Ball would be proud of. I loved every second of it!

DELL: You're physically incapable of disliking anything.

BERT: The one, lonely tissue I had in my pocket was so drenched by the end I could have made it into a papier-mâché hand puppet.

DELL: I love you darling.

If only you were that rotten little critic at *The Mirror*.

BERT: Who cares about that rotten little critic at *The Mirror*?

DELL: I care about the that rotten little critic at *The Mirror*.

JUDY: There's nothing you can do about that rotten little critic at *The Mirror*.

BERT: Where is the woman who pointed him out to me and said 'I wouldn't micturate on him if he were aflame!'?

DELL: She's here. I wouldn't.

BERT: The audience love it! They love Toni Lamond.
How was last night? Did they love Toni Lamond?
DELL: I don't go every night.
BERT: You don't?
DELL: Maybe I do.
BERT: Did they enjoy it?
DELL: They loved it. They loved Toni Lamond.
BERT: Of course they did.
And in any case, four million people watched your Alzheimer's eps.
Four million.
JUDY: Let's take this angst. This loathing. This contempt.
Let's take it all and channel it into the work today.
How about this? Frank hasn't put on a show in a few years, is it time for him to don some greasepaint?
BERT: Supplied by Cookie … so it's paint paint—
DELL: And doesn't come off?
JUDY: And after all the drama of getting the drama on the stage—
BERT: Frank gives the performance of his life as Nathan Detroit to Shirl's Adelaide in *Guys and Dolls*—
And then! Councillor Muldoon gets a new position at the *Burrigan Examiner* in which the power will immediately go to his head?
JUDY: THEATRE CRITIC.
BERT: BAH, BAH, BUMMMM.
JUDY: And as the Wandin Valley Dramatic Society await their reviews—
DELL: Still high after an opening night triumph—
BERT: Muldoon slams them.
JUDY: And Shirley gets under the pyramid with a voodoo doll and wishes a slow, violent death for him.
BERT: You love killing.
JUDY: I do not! Why does everyone think I love killing?
BERT: You do. You love it. You wanna marry killing. You wanna have killing's babies. You wanna grow old with killing and retire with killing and buy a caravan with killing and travel around Australia in the caravan killing.
DELL: Darlings, I'm sorry to go all Barbra Streisand and rain on your parade—
BERT: Jim will never let us kill Muldoon.

DELL: Isn't there another character we could make a theatre critic and get Judy to kill?

This has been a riff between friends and colleagues, yet BERT *still writes a bunch of it down. They have LOTS OF STORIES they have to come up with week after week.*

JUDY *takes the paper from* DELL *and tears the offending pages up.*

God I hope we're killing someone today.

BERT: I think we might be killing someone today.

JUDY: We're not.

BERT: Think about it.

JUDY: Think about what?

BERT: It's a special meeting. When did Jim call you both to be here?

JUDY *and* DELL: Last night.

BERT: Exactly.

JUDY: What do you mean, 'exactly'?

BERT: What I mean is something's going on. I reckon someone wants to leave the show.

Jim gets you two in, together, for the big stuff.

DELL: I did hear that Lorrae wants to do a musical.

JUDY: For god's sake.

BERT: Lorrae's not going to leave a job where she gets to sit on her bum making excellently penned wisecracks and drinking tea all day.

DELL: Would you want to have to pretend Brian's a delightful and sexy companion day in day out?

JUDY: She really is an incredible actress, isn't she?

BERT: Brian's alright—

DELL: Come to think of it—Penny was very wistful at my opening the other night.

JUDY: How so?

DELL: She wants to be making plays in her little theatre.

JUDY: Her little theatre has eighty seats and this show is its great patron.

Penny's not going anywhere.

BERT: After she has the twins, what else is there for Vicki to do?

DELL: I beg your pardon, Berto!

JUDY: Are you asking what else is there for Vicki to do after she's birthed babies?

BERT: Well, yeah, she's had the romance, she's having the babies—what else can we have her do? I'm just saying, the dramatic possibilites in a television serial—

DELL: I have a notebook full of things she can do, Berto. A notebook full. Look at this notebook. I need a new notebook it's so notebook-full of ideas for new things she can do.

A woman's life doesn't end when she has babies.

BERT: Of course a woman's—I'm not saying—I'm just saying the dramatic possibilities—

JUDY: Dry up?

DELL: They certainly do bloody not Bert.

JUDY: No drama for mummy?

I finished having babies seventeen years ago and I wish to Aspasia herself the storylines would slow down in my life—

DELL: I finished having babies thirty years ago and I've got drama knocking on my door from dawn to dusk!

Every day, drama! Old drama from the past! New drama beckoning from a wink in a café, a slapped bum at the swimming pool!

JUDY: Who slapped your bum at the swimming pool?

DELL: Whose bum did I slap at the swimming pool?

JUDY: And weren't you just telling me your own wife has gone on an adventure with Hoges up north?

DELL: Oooh! Look out, Berto!

Hoges and Noelene haven't been happy for years! Hoges is forever on the look out.

He was outrageous at the Logies!

JUDY: That man could flirt for Australia.

Maybe a cool American blonde like Evelyn is just Hoges' style.

DELL: And Berto, I don't need to tell you how enticingly Hoges fills out a pair of stubbies.

BERT: It's a fill-um, Dell. Surely they've bought him some trousers.

DELL: Drama doesn't dry up after babies, Berto. It ramps up to an almost nuclear level.

Your Evelyn hasn't had a baby in twenty years and she's about to run off with Hoges!

How obscenely fabulous!

Enter SALLY *(twenties). She's laden with textbooks, newspapers, pamphlets, medical journals. She's in a nurse's uniform.*

BERT: Sally!

SALLY: Oh. Judy.

I didn't realise we were killing someone.

JUDY: Hello to you too, Sally.

SALLY: I didn't bring my fatals cheat sheet.

I had barely any notice for this meeting, and no-one mentioned I needed to bring my fatals cheat sheet.

Oh jeez.

BERT: Which ward were you on last night?

SALLY: Geriatrics.

Lots of poo and war stories.

BERT: I prefer it when you're in emergency.

SALLY: There's still poo in emergency.

BERT: It's a more frantic faecal adventure, though, isn't it?

SALLY: Poo is poo, when you're at the end of it like I am.

Should I run home and get my fatals sheet?

BERT: What makes you think we're killing someone?

SALLY: Judy, of course.

Jim's not calling in Judy from Berry for a salmonella outbreak at the Wandin Valley Tombola—

JUDY: You can die from salmonella, can't you?

SALLY: It's very rare.

I've got the stats here, if you're interested?

DELL: I don't think we've had a tombola in a while—

SALLY: Health Department writes to Jim constantly about it.

I'm sure he'd love us to do it.

Undercooked eggs … unpasteurised milk … raw meat, chook, seafood?

It's actually a proper public service storyline.

BERT: Maybe Esme hasn't done the right thing with eggs for her award-winning pav?

DELL: She would never.

BERT: Here's an offer:

Esme's babysitting Chloe one arvo, turns her back and Chloe's into the pav.

Chloe starts getting sicker and sicker.

She goes out to the chook pen to sleep on the soft straw, among the chickens.

Esme finds her. Blue lipped. Eyes staring straight ahead.

Dead! Of pavlova!

JUDY: What is wrong with you?

I can't be part of killing Chloe. She's named after my daughter.

We're not killing Chloe.

DELL: We're not killing Chloe.

JUDY: And, how could we do that to Molly and Brendan?

DELL: We've put Molly and Brendan through enough.

BERT: Let's put them through some more! See how much they can take?

DELL: You're a sicko.

BERT: I love seeing good-looking young people suffer.

Love it.

JUDY: You're a sicko!

BERT: Says the woman who offed their baby.

DELL: We're not killing Simon either.

No disposing of characters named after our kids, got it?

JUDY: How is Simon, Dell?

DELL: He's okay, darl. Thanks for asking.

JUDY: Of course.

DELL: Most people don't ask.

JUDY: Most people are idiots.

DELL: Aren't they?

JUDY: Is he happy?

DELL: He's always been a happy kid.

JUDY: That's what matters, doesn't it?

DELL: It does.

JUDY: [*a new thought*] Listen.

I told Jim after Christopher I couldn't kill anyone for a really long time.

In your parlance, Dell, I was *emphatique.*

I didn't even want to kill Christopher.

BERT: But you did.

JUDY: I had to.

BERT: You *had* to?

JUDY: I did what I had to do.

SALLY: What happened?

DELL: Listen, and learn, young Sally.

JUDY: Jim called me up and said, 'I need you in Sydney to kill Molly's baby Christopher.'

I said, 'Jim, I don't kill babies.'

He said, 'Of course you kill babies. You love killing babies. You live for killing babies.'

I said, 'I don't kill Molly and Brendan's babies. Those babies are my babies. Brendan and Molly are Barry and me. I don't kill their babies.'

To which he said, 'How about I send you a case of 1971 Penfolds Grange?'

BERT: I thought it was just one or two!

JUDY: A case.

DELL: He sends you a case of Penfolds Grange …

SALLY: A case?!

BERT: A case!

A tiny beat.

JUDY: So I killed the baby.

They all laugh.

BERT: I wonder what he'll offer you this time—

JUDY: I earned every bottle.

DELL: And you did it beautifully.

Molly falling off the ladder … Brendan blaming her for Christopher's death—my god, how very dare he—I couldn't see the TV I was crying so much.

You're the only Golden Teardrop Winner in this room for a reason.

Enter SHARON *(twenties or forties)—in full motorcycle gear. Full rock star/former jail inmate vibes.*

She makes sure the door is closed behind her. She doesn't want anyone else in the building hearing what's about to go down.

She comes in singing like it's a fanfare. Her swearing is not to be milked for cheap laughs—it's the way she thinks and processes.

SHARON: LET'S MAKE SOME TEE VEE TODAY
LET'S MAKE SOME TEE VEE TODAY
LET'S GET THOSE RATINGS SKY HIGH
LET'S MAKE THE PUNTERS ALL CRY
LET'S MAKE SOME TEE VEE TODAY
MY MATES!
Big fucken day, team!

She goes to the bar fridge, grabs a Coke, guzzles it down.

The ratings!

Christ on a shiny new Harley bike—Sally, you're a genius!

Leprosy! The punters! They bloody love the leprosy!

Who'd have thought?

Sally thought, that's who! Have we ever head a medical advisor, who's also a story genius?

Jim's stoked. The network's stoked.

Leprosy Association people are stoked!

Let's have some hearty applause for Sally!

They all clap.

You all had your coffee?

Got your ciggies?

Got your pens and your crazy and your tellie gold dust magic at the ready?

I've got some news mates.

Some big fucken news.

Direct from Jim last night.

I've been fanging around the city since trying to figure out what we do.

It's—what do those fuckwit publicity people say when something's a big secret? Dell?

DELL: Embargoed?

SHARON: Yeah mates. This shit is fully embargoed.

No telling anything to anyone.

Not your husbands, your wives, your kids, your friends, your nieces, your nephews … you can't even purr it into the ears of your American Shorthair cat.

Sally you're a cat person, aren't you?

SALLY: Yes Shaz, I'm a cat person.

SHARON: I can pick it. Every time. Don't breathe a word to that cagey little fucker.

DELL: Darling get on with it please?

SHARON *lights a ciggie.*

SHARON: Mates. I don't even know if the show survives it—

JUDY: Bloody hell Shazza—what is it?

SHARON: We'll make sure we survive it, but shit.

I seriously dunno if after we do this we're all begging *Sons and Daughters* for jobs.

JUDY: I don't want to go to *Sons and Daughters*.

DELL: *Sons and Daughters*?

BERT: No-one wants to go to *Sons and Daughters*.

Sips some more coke. Smokes some more ciggie.

SHARON: Annie wants to leave the show.

An enormous beat.

They're all shocked. This is BIG NEWS.

JUDY *grabs her bag and goes to leave.*

SHARON: Oy! Judy! Where do you think you're going?

JUDY: I'm not killing Molly.

DELL: You can't make us kill Molly.

JUDY: I won't do it.

SHARON: Who said anything about killing her?

JUDY: In five years on this show I've never been called in on a Tuesday.

SHARON: There's nothing to say she couldn't piss off to a year-long hippy love-in at a Bangladeshi ashram, is there?

I bloody well doubt she would, but we're not putting any ideas in the bin yet.

JUDY: Jim can't let her leave.

SHARON: Apparently she's feeling like she doesn't know where she ends and Molly begins.

JUDY: What's this show without Molly?

SHARON: No show is one person, mate.

JUDY: Annie is our biggest star.

They love her—whether they're seven or seventeen or seventy.

SHARON: Jim's offered more screen time.

Less screen time.

Told her she can have time off every year for a movie or a play or a Kennedy Miller mini-series.

He's offered her more cash than any of us typewriting paddle-pops will ever see in our lives—

Turned it all down.

She wants an out she can't come back from.

JUDY: Have you spoken to Annie?

SHARON: It's not my place, mate.

JUDY: Told her what this means for the show? For her colleagues? For us?

SHARON: Her contract's up, she doesn't want to renew it.

JUDY: I don't think she knows what it's like out there.

SHARON: 'Out there'?

JUDY: You don't either, Shaz.

DELL: Jude's right, Shaz.

JUDY: You've only worked here.

DELL: The three of us have worked on all the other shows.

JUDY: And believe me: this is an all expenses paid holiday to a resort on the Gold Coast. Every other show I've worked on is a thirty-year-old mouldy caravan at Sussex Inlet.

SHARON: And what's wrong with Sussex Inlet?

JUDY: It's okay, but it's no Surfer's Paradise resort drinking piña coladas in the pool.

Jim lets us write what we like.

DELL: He bribes us with Penfolds instead of Miranda Spumante.

BERT: Did you know *Sons and Daughters'* Christmas party had home-brand sausage rolls and Miranda Spumante?

JUDY: She needs to know this.

BERT: Someone needs to tell her.

DELL: Save her from a life of Miranda Spumante! The horror!

SHARON: Listen I'm all for locking her in her dressing room after each day's shoot— Jim won't let me.

A beat.

JUDY: We can't. We just can't. It's unthinkable.

BERT: So we're going to kill her?

SHARON: Look, I'll be straight with you.

We're not *not* going to kill her.

We can try to find a way to get her out of the show forever without killing her, but my gut feeling is she's a goner.

DELL: Molly, Brendan and Chloe leaving to go backpacking around South America?

SHARON: Shane Withington's staying.

DELL: Thank god—the show really couldn't do with losing both of them.

BERT: For now, I'll wager.

JUDY: Could we have them subletting the farm to a new tree-changing family?

BERT: A peaceful transition of power between greenies at Jones Farm.

SHARON: What a ratings bonanza.

Just Molly's going. I repeat: Brendan and Chloe are staying.

A beat.

Jim wants us to milk the pink tits out of it like it's five a.m. in the last dairy left after mad cow disease has killed every other cow in the country.

It'll run over the fourteen weeks before peak ratings.

BERT: We'd be killing her over fourteen weeks?

SHARON: Fourteen weeks, mates.

JUDY: Ah, so fourteen weeks to convince her to stay?

SHARON: I love your optimism, Jude-oh, but good luck.

JUDY: Is Jim open to her changing her mind?

SHARON: He'd be stoked if she did—

BERT: Convince her to stay, Jude, he might buy you a vineyard!

SHARON: It's not gonna happen.

BERT: Any ideas from Jim on how he'd like to see her cark it?

JUDY: Bert!

SHARON: He wants us to keep in mind how many kids watch the show.

We get about a hundred fan letters a day. Seventy of them will be for Annie. And most of them from kids.

Let's not scar them too hard … but let's scar them a bit, you know?

JUDY: The kids in town are always asking me about Molly and Doris the pig.

They love her because Annie plays her with such fun and fight—

SHARON: Dressed like she's going to the circus.

SALLY: An accident, then?

Short, sharp, an opportunity to teach about the randomness of life?

SHARON: Steady on mate, we're not brainstorming yet.

We need to talk a few things through.

Everyone with a TV watches this show.

SALLY: My brother doesn't.

SHARON: Well your brother's a fucken drongo.

You think those *Sons and Daughters* hacks down the hall have looked down the barrel of anything like this?

No-one would give a shit if Pat the Rat was blown up inside her limo on the way to the races one day—

JUDY: And she's definitely going?

SHARON: Annie's off to be a movie star.

JUDY: Definitely, definitively, absolutely?

SHARON: Or a sculptor. Or fuck knows what.

She doesn't want to be your Molly Jones anymore.

JUDY: I feel like I'm being dumped.

DELL: You are being dumped.

JUDY: After everything I've done.

Didn't I give her the best storylines?

If I could just speak to her? Tell her how I feel?

SHARON: Mate if you're auditioning to replace her you're doing a bloody good job—

BERT: What's the plan for today then?

SHARON: We're going to come up with a few ideas and figure out if they work: for Annie, for the show, for the audience, for the ratings, for Jim.

I've been pitching a big moment like this the whole time I've been here.

JUDY: This is your idea? To kill her?

SHARON: I've been wanting to off someone big for years.

I had my eye on one of those bozos in the club.

JUDY: Why does it have to be Molly?

SHARON: She doesn't want to be able to come back.

JUDY: She might think that now.

DELL: How old is she?

JUDY: Just thirty. She's a baby.

BERT: Thirty's old.

Oh, Bert.

DELL: She might think she doesn't want to come back, but it's hard out there for any actor.

JUDY: Let alone an actor who's a national sweetheart for one role.

DELL: She'll want to come back.

BERT: A thirty-year-old actress. I mean—thirty's old for an actress—

DELL: Oh, Bert. Shoosh now.

JUDY: Let's leave it open for her to come back. No killing.

DELL: Surely we can come up with something that feels permanent for Annie, is good for ratings and doesn't need a funeral episode?

SHARON: It's completely open, mate.

This is what we pay you the slightly higher than award rate for.

A beat.

You wanna break for half an hour?

Have a coffee? Have a ciggie? Have a Mintie or seven? Have a think?

BERT: Sounds good.

SHARON: Any idea goes, too.

Let's think big.

Or, let's think small. Intimate. Personal. Heart shit.

SALLY: Want me to start researching heart disease?

SHARON: No mate, I mean heart shit as in emotional.

Stabs at the heart. Metaphorically.

But sure, kid, knock yourself out, maybe it's a heart attack?

SALLY: Women do actually die of heart attacks at a rate no-one is talking about—

SHARON: Here's my two bob is: if this is gonna work—it needs to be big, or fucken heartbreakingly truthful.

Let's also think about whether we might use it as an opportunity to do some good out there for the punters—I dunno what, but you know, like those *Mates* episodes showed Australia what absolute tools they are to homos.

Like those leprosy episodes showed them it's not a disease from the Bible.

Like Vicki's wedding showed everyone it's possible to have your hand up a cow's arse then be in a wedding dress an hour later.

They each go to a part of the room to begin working. There's smoking. There's coffee.

BERT, *with his notepad and pencil, grabs some headphones and sits by the sound system. Puts a cassette in and off he goes.*

DELL *sits at the table, gets out scripts and notes and rifles through them. Stopping to think and jot things down.*

SALLY *exits and brings back more medical books. Reads them intently.*

SHARON *paces around the room, stopping only when inspo strikes, to write something furiously on her note pad.*

JUDY *dreams, makes notes. Dreams, makes notes.*

The half-hour passes. Each of them has been doing their writing and thinking and smoking and coffee-ing and Mintie-ing.

SHARON *looks at her watch.*

Oy, Sally. Go over to the phone and call triple-oh!

SALLY: Oh god, what's happened?

SHARON: We're about to commit a murder …

JUDY: I thought you said we didn't have to kill her—

BERT: How brave is she, in an industry like this, to leave a show like this?

SHARON: Brave, or stupid?

What a wicket!

Biggest star on the biggest show in Australia.

Can pay her mortgage. Can pay all her bills.

Could go to Hawaii over Christmas break and fly to Noosa every other weekend if she wanted.

Why you wouldn't set and forget on that, I don't know.

Actors are all fucken mental.

JUDY: I know why she'd want to leave.

SHARON: Someone's coming around—

JUDY: I'm not coming around. I get it.

Why does Dell write plays? Why do I write poems for obscure literary mags?

SHARON: Tell me, mate. Also, did you just say 'pomes' instead of 'po-ems'? Have I been saying 'poems' wrong my whole life?

JUDY: I said 'poems'.

SHARON: There! Again! Am I taking crazy pills? You heard it didn't you, Bert? She says 'pomes'.

JUDY: Do you want to know why she wants to move on?

SHARON: I'm stoked to go to a job every day where we get to make up stories.

That people actually watch.

Try working in the laundry room at Silverwater and you'll know what a good job is and isn't!

DELL: How many people did you kill before television saved you from jail, Shaz? What was your best prison weapon? How many women did you see dispatched on the laundry shift? Tell the kids at home how you went from being Australia's Most Wanted to Australia's Most Wanted Story Boss on Australia's Most Loved TV show?

JUDY: Annie's an artist, Shaz.

SHARON: She's paid to learn lines and look good.

DELL: Darling, actors and actresses are so much more than people who learn lines and look good.

BERT: The good ones are—

JUDY: It's an act of bravery.

To stand in front of people you don't know and be inside someone else's skin—

DELL: All while having to forget a camera is up your nose?

None of us could do that.

SHARON: I reckon I could.

Just wouldn't want to.

All that waiting. Waiting for a job. Waiting for the lights to be ready on set. Waiting for Esme to have the right cardigan.

I'll stay here in the engine room, thanks, where we decide what shit happens to which unlucky bastard this week.

DELL: You've got a great face for TV.

SHARON: For *Prisoner*. Imagine a mug like this on our show?

Any of youse ever been actors?

JUDY: God no.
BERT: In sketches on the radio, never near a camera.
SALLY: I've spent a lot of time in theatres.
Do operating theatres count?
BERT: Sally just made a nursing joke! Ten out of ten, Sally!
SALLY: Thank you Bert, thank you.
SHARON: How about you, Dell?
You've got a bit of an actress flourish to you?
You're good looking enough to be one.
DELL: I thought, like you, about a hundred years ago, that any silly duffer could do it.
I was writing on a Crawfords cop show and getting sick of actors flubbing my lines.
Somehow I convinced the producer I could guest on my episode: Prostitute Number One.
It was hard, I was terrible. Couldn't forget the camera was there.
Turns out they weren't flubbing my lines.
I wasn't writing any good lines.
JUDY: Annie's a big talent. I guess it makes sense she's ready to move on.
She needs to be doing new things.
Safety for an artist can feel like a type of death.
SHARON: Says the woman who knows TV death better than anyone—
Righto then.
Who wants to kick things off?

SHARON *goes to the butchers paper with a pen. She makes some sort of note of every idea.*

Before we get specific, I reckon we should nut out the pros and cons of keeping her in the land of the living versus whacking her.
JUDY: 'Whacking her'? Sharon.
SHARON: Terminating her? Slaying her? Liquidating her?
Having her meet the only inevitability of being a human being?
DELL: TV characters can live forever.
JUDY: That's why I love doing this.
To keep people alive forever?
It's impossible in real life, here we can?

SHARON: You kill anyone they let you at for a bottle of fizz!

JUDY: I don't enjoy it, Shaz.
Every death takes something from me.

SHARON: If she lives, we have to send her away somehow. What's in it for the show?

JUDY: Obviously, she can come back.

BERT: We can bring the character back, at the very least.

JUDY: You mean, with a different actress?

DELL: We don't do that on this show.

BERT: We're the only ones who don't.

SHARON: They're about to do it on *Sons and Daughters* with Belinda Giblin playing Rowena's character.
Let's see how that goes, fucken pikelets.

BERT: There's no reason we couldn't do it here.

JUDY: Annie's singular.

DELL: If she leaves Brendan and Chloe, we get all sorts of abandonment storylines.
Especially as Chloe gets older.

JUDY: Brendan will have trust issues.

BERT: A rubbish partner to anyone new until he finds 'the one' again.

DELL: If there's a mystery around it, we can tease it out over the years.
'Where's Molly?'—it's catchy.

BERT: 'Where's Molly?' *is* catchy.

SHARON: It's not our show.
We don't do murder mysteries. Kidnapping mysteries. We don't really do mysteries.

JUDY: Shaz's right. It's not the world of the show.

SHARON: It's not Jim's world. People don't get murdered or go missing in Jim's world.

JUDY: What could possibly happen to Molly that she'd leave her husband and her child?

SHARON: Brendan could cheat?

JUDY: Shane would never agree to it.

DELL: And would he?
Would Brendan ever cheat on Molly?

JUDY: Not our Brendan and Molly.

DELL: Do we make another Brendan and Molly?

Do they start to show cracks?

Does Brendan fall in love with a patient, like he fell in love with Molly?

JUDY: Why would Molly leave Chloe with him?!

SALLY: I know: there's a way she could go that would make sense for her to be away from them.

And would work in well with the show. It's social, and medical.

SHARON: Love it when our nursey inserts some science!

SALLY: Anecdotally, for a long time now, we've thought there was a link between cannabis and triggering schizophrenia and there's a couple of studies just out that seem to solidify this.

It's mostly in young men, but not always.

SHARON: If anyone's going to be smashing cones, it's Molly—

DELL: It is—

BERT: Artistic temperament. Open-minded.

SHARON: Choofy choof!

DELL: Loves the farm.

SALLY: She could grow some marijuana as pain relief for, say, Bob's bad back—

DELL: She tries some—

SALLY: And it triggers a psychosis—

BERT: We get a few eps of her growing madness—

DELL: We get the pros and cons of cannabis use, but also the risks—

SHARON: She goes Molly-mad-snake and has to be carted away to Burrigan in a straightjacket!

BERT: Or she walks off into the bush and is never seen again! *Picnic at Hanging Rock*-style?

SHARON: In the nuddy! Ratings!

They all laugh.

All ideas welcome, mates!

SALLY: Let's leave it up though.

Schizophrenia gets a bad rap in shows like ours and we could look at a more sensitive portrayal of it.

SHARON: It's a 'fuck yeah' to schizophrenia!

JUDY: Did Annie have any suggestions?

SHARON: I love ideas from the actrines.

JUDY: They know their characters, Shazzy.

BERT: Sometimes their ideas are better than ours.

SHARON: But mostly our ideas are better than theirs.

Annie thinks Molly could get involved in some sort of cult … She leaves to be on some mountain with them.

BERT: Brendan and Chloe could follow when Shane gets jack of doing the show without Annie?

SHARON: Where's the drama in that?

JUDY: Seeing your wife get brainwashed by someone and leaving you?

BERT: We could get Bruce Spence to play the cult leader.

DELL: Would you follow Bruce Spence up a mountain?

BERT: He may be interesting of face, Dell, but he's tall of body and tall of body and interesting of face is quite the combo for a cult leader. Rasputin was tall of body, interesting of face. Brought down an empire!

SHARON: So we've got Molly goes skitso.

SALLY: 'Develops schizophrenia.'

SHARON: Follows Bruce Spence up a hill.

Have we got any ideas on how to keep Molly alive that don't involve her going fucken batshit?

BERT: Molly is a bit batty. That's why everyone loves her.

JUDY: Annie would love that storyline, I'll bet.

BERT: Actors love going cuckoo.

JUDY: Cuckoo means she can come back.

SALLY: Guys, I don't mean to be that annoying person, but I don't think we call people cuckoo anymore. Or skitso.

We call them mentally ill.

SHARON: Is bonkers okay?

SALLY: No, Shaz. Bonkers is not okay.

SHARON: Next idea!

JUDY: This is a show with a feminist undertone.

SHARON: That's one F-word I wouldn't be saying outside this room, Judy.

JUDY: It is, that's what happens when you're on a show with mostly women writers, Shaz.

There's an opportunity here to really look at where women are today.

Before she met Brendan, before she came to Wandin Valley, Molly was a career girl. A fashion designer.

That's a fast life. A life of colour and fun and creativity and money and parties.

We know she loves the farm, sure. But she came from a big, wild, fun life in the city.

I know she writes for the paper sometimes and she loves to chain herself to a tree, but essentially, we've got her running the farm and running the house while Brendan goes to work at the hospital. Doing most, not all, but most of Chloe's care.

Think about it: we've ended up putting her in a pretty traditional housewife role.

There's a couple of women in my town who are like this: they had big city lives, and actually did the whole 'move to the country' thing.

DELL: It's your story.

JUDY: I suppose it is.

DELL: Of course it is. You and Barry are Molly and Brendan.

That's why the audience cares about them.

JUDY: My friend Barbara—she's a sculptor. She and her husband bought a block and moved from the city. It's got a shed out the back where she can do her work. He opened the grocery shop next to our video shop. Over the five years they've been there, three more kids came along. The shop got busier. The kids needed more.

The sculpting shed started being used more for junk storage. Her work slipped further and further down their list of priorities.

Then one day, the shop's closed. And another day. And another day.

Barry goes around to see if something's up, and Barbara's husband's in bed and the kids are a mess.

Barbara had had an invite from the National Art School. She'd gone up to the city for her two weeks, and decided she wasn't coming back.

DELL: Who hasn't dreamed about leaving her kids and getting her old life back?

SALLY: Why? I can't imagine—

DELL: Just you wait, young Sally! How long have you been married?

SALLY: Two years.

DELL: Wait until you have kids.

SALLY: It's the eighties, Dell. The blokes help now.

DELL: That's what I thought in the sixties.

Even if your Russell is the first man in the history of men to share it all with you, there will come a time when you'll just want yourself to yourself.

You'll want your body to be your own—not a feeding, hugging, comforting apparatus for your kids and husband.

Your own.

Don't worry love, barely anyone acts on the feelings. Society will scorn! Children will be psychologically damaged for life!

But you'll think about it one day when you just want to sleep in for five more bloody minutes—

SALLY: I don't want to hear this Dell.

DELL: I'm just preparing you love.

SALLY: Can you prepare me another day?

SALLY *shows a crinkled ultrasound picture. Everyone gets excited.*

DELL: What's this? I need my glasses—

JUDY: How exciting! Congratulations darling.

SALLY: We've been trying for such a long time—

BERT: Congratulations!

DELL: Then don't listen to grizzled old me, sweetheart—how wonderful!

BERT: And they give you the ultrasound picture now?

SHARON: When are you due mate?

SALLY: Not for ages.

SHARON: You'll recommend someone else when you have the baby?

SALLY: No I won't be recommending someone else when I have the baby, Shazza.

Russell's going to have the baby when I'm working. I'll be here.

SHARON: Well that's very fucken modern Sally.

DELL: Maybe it will be different for you girls?

SHARON: Righto breeders—let's get back to it.

Jude was telling us about her mates with the grocery store and the shed that got used for junk instead of making shit no-one ever bought—

JUDY: So Barbara, the sculptor, who did sell work, as it happened, left her family.

I saw her last time I was here. She's got a bedsit in the Cross. She feels like the lights are back on.

She's making great work.

She's having love affairs with twenty-three-year-old painters—who go home to their sharehouses and sleep on mattresses without fitted sheets.

DELL: Young men really can be deliciously revolting, can't they?

JUDY: She looks alive again.

BERT: How are the kids?

JUDY: Not sure about the kids. Who knows how they'll be?

BERT: The husband?

JUDY: Come on, Berto. Men move on in about half an hour.

There's always a Carol with a cauliflower casserole and a warm pair of boozies to comfort them.

DELL: There's a narrative around women leaving the family that isn't the same as when a man leaves his family.

JUDY: Here's my offer: there's a lot we can mine with a storyline like Barbara's for Molly.

We could grow her sense of despair over the weeks prior.

And when she goes—leaving Brendan and Chloe behind—

It could almost be this great catharsis for the Australian women stuck at home dreaming they could do it too.

Imagine!

DELL: I love it Jude.

SHARON: Of course you love it—

BERT: I do too!

SHARON: This is a show about community and family.

We need to think pretty carefully about making a hero out of a mother who leaves her kid.

JUDY: Why?

Why not try and shift the conversation?

Show some compassion to the women who do this and are ostracised forever for it?

No-one ostracises a man for moving to Queensland.

No-one even chases him for child support.

DELL: Ha! Child support. Child support is a myth.

SHARON: Leaving your kids means you're one of life's great shitburgers.

JUDY: This life is a short one, Shaz.

DELL: We all want freedom and a life, don't we?

It's a brave move.

Your friend Barbara is a brave woman.

JUDY: She sure is.

SHARON: Sounds like a selfish arsehole to me.

JUDY: It's epidemic in men. Leave the wife and family when it's all too much.

See the kids every second weekend and for a week in school holidays.

Have a new family they'll likely abandon again when the going gets tough.

We don't ever talk about the damage a man's leaving his family does to his kids.

SHARON: Because it's as common as a headache the morning after a piss-up. My dad left us when I was three. Had a few more families.

Still welcome at the pub.

DELL: So did mine—when I was eleven.

JUDY: And no-one bat an eyelid, I'll bet.

SHARON: We were better without him, truth be told. Boozer.

JUDY: There's five of us in this room, two can relate to this story.

SALLY: Three.

JUDY: Three.

SHARON: Aren't we showing it's more likely Brendan would go for ciggies and never come back?

JUDY: Where it's interesting, Shaz, is we get to talk about the issues inside marriages that lead to a woman feeling desperate enough to leave.

Where is that happening on our TVs?

DELL: Molly would be perfect for it. So would Vicki, actually. So would Shirley.

JUDY: Because we've created characters who make decisions about their own lives.

DELL: And women dream about having their own lives away from it all. Every now and then.

BERT: Matron's got the vibe of someone who left her kids, don't you think?

DELL: For a thrilling life of roster management at the Wandin Valley hospital!

A beat. They all think this over.

SHARON: When Molly wears a pair of purple overalls, the shops all sell out of purple overalls.

DELL: Exactly.

SHARON: Do you want us to set off a generation of mothers thinking it's okay to clear out on their kids?

JUDY: What if what we set off was a bunch of blokes watching, thinking, 'I don't want that to happen to me', and what we actually do is help people to be more thoughtful inside their marriages?

DELL: Then, a year or two down the track, if the good theatre and movie roles don't materialise for Annie—

BERT: Maybe Molly comes back—

JUDY: On her own terms—

DELL: Brendan's found a new wife, she's basically mother to Chloe—

JUDY: And we have a whole slew of storylines around Molly's re-entry, Brendan and Molly's undeniable chemistry, Chloe's reticence to let her mother back in.

DELL: Put it up, Shaz. It's a great storyline. Put it up.

She does so.

I would have loved to have left my kids to write plays in a dinky little bedsit in Kings Cross.

I'd have had an Italian espresso coffee in an actual cafe every morning or maybe a swim in the ocean?

I'd have a lover for every night of the week—some old, who knew how pleasure works … some young, I could teach how pleasure works.

The new Dell Brehon play would be kicking Arthur Miller out of the theatres.

Who was it who said 'The enemy of art is the pram in the hallway?'

Single mother to three kids and no skills but these meant a lot of episodes of radio soaps and articles about movie stars meant much less time on the Great Australian Play. Great Australian plays.

JUDY: I got so lucky with Barry.
He's at the shop all day. Chasing late fees so I can sit at my desk and write.
DELL: You are lucky.
JUDY: I wish every woman was.
DELL: You're the only one I know, Jude.
BERT: I'm lucky too. With Evelyn.
DELL: Of course you are, Berto.
You're a bloke.
Most blokes are doing just fine in this department.
Could Evelyn say the same thing?
BERT: I think Evelyn loves being a wife and a mother—
DELL: Really?
BERT: She doesn't want for anything—
JUDY: She obviously wants for something Berto, she's in Darwin sipping cocktails at the Kakadu Inn with Hoges!
DELL: Is she happy?

A beat.

BERT: I actually don't know.
DELL: And you're one of the good ones, Bert!
SHARON: Jim'll never go for Molly leaving them.
JUDY: Jim's production company is called JNP Productions—James and Philippa Productions.
He's someone deeply invested in the happiness of his wife.
SHARON: Okay.
But where are the tears in this scenario?
JUDY: If we build the scaffolding properly, Shaz, they're everywhere!
For Brendan, for Chloe, for Molly.
For every woman who hasn't lived the life she wants.
DELL: Which is pretty much every woman watching.
BERT: 'You're every woman it's all in you—'
DELL: 'Anything you want done baby I'll do it naturally—'
BERT: I saw Chaka Khan once. At a dive bar in Chicago!
SALLY: Why were you in a dive bar in Chicago?
BERT: Johnny used to send me around looking for new comedians.
SALLY: Who's Johnny?

DELL: What?! Bert hasn't told you eighty-seven times he worked on the Johnny Carson show?

JUDY: And *I Love Lucy*.

DELL: And Graham Kennedy.

BERT: And now, I'm but a humble joke writer on *A Country Practice*.
Who once boogied hard to Chaka Khan live in a dive bar in Chicago.

SHARON: Who the fuck is Chaka Khan?

SALLY: Surely you weren't in the slammer that long, Shaz!

SHARON: Just having yas on.
Also, Sally, we don't call it the slammer, we call it the Women's Correctional Facility.

JUDY: By the time the show comes on—it's seven-thirty.
Our female demo have spent their whole day doing everything for everyone else.
The escape this storyline would bring them. Into the living rooms where they're living this stuff!
Revolutionary!

SHARON: It'd also make Molly a national villain.
Not sure Annie'll enjoy that when she's out buying her lamb chops for tea in her new life.

She writes on the board: 'Molly splits, home revolution'

Any more suggestions for Molly's exit that don't involve a funeral?

BERT: What about her mother getting sick, her going to look after the mother, and she never comes back?

DELL: Bert you just stole my life story.

BERT: Oh, Dell, so I did.
Why didn't you ever go back?

DELL: I couldn't afford to.

BERT: Did he ever come out here?

DELL: He thought Australie sounded tres awful!

BERT: Would you go back now?

DELL: God no, he's had about six new children since we all left.
Four new mothers.

BERT: Frenchies, eh?
Don't know what they're missing.
Molly's mother gets sick, she goes back to the city—

SHARON: Fuck me dead, Berto.
Molly's *mother* getting sick? Snoozeville.
But of course, no bad ideas mate and all that.

It's time. To explore the inevitable.

SHARON *dramatically writes 'DEAD MOLLY' on the butchers paper.*

Number one—We all love a death. Punters love a death.

Number two—punters suspecting their favourite character is gonna kark it means lots of angry letters. Lots of angry letters remind us how much they love the show and that makes us feel warm all through our fast-declining middle-aged bodies.

Number three—tears mates tears. Don't you want to make Australia cry like a baby with blocked ears on a long haul flight between here and London? Tears that actually hurt, mates. That really fucken hurt.

Number four—all of the above means big, huge, insanely expensive advertising dollars. Happy boss, we keep jobs that bit longer.

JUDY: But, Molly?
Do we really want to kill Molly?

SHARON: She's the one leaving.

JUDY: She's a young mum with everything to live for.

SHARON: Exactly.
It's a slow, sensual, televisual orgasm.

A beat.

We've made Wandin Valley into a cosy lefty utopia and we all think they're real people and it's a real place.

We're afraid to let them get in the dirt.

DELL: Simon and Vicki are literally in the dirt in the opening credits.

SHARON: The shit that goes down on this show never happens to our leads.

JUDY: Molly's miscarrying Christopher so late in the day was pretty huge.

SHARON: If we choose the right death, the punters can be part of it—
It'll be an 'is she going to croak or isn't she?' situation?
They'll be begging us to save her.

SALLY: And what if … what if there's a chance of really, truly educating the country about some condition or disease we haven't done before?

That people really need to know about?

They look at DELL.

BERT *saves them all from the pain of what they're looking at her for.*

BERT: Here's a pitch:

JUDY *and* DELL *are starting to come around to the fact that Molly's death might be an inevitability.*

It's Mozart's birthday—

This is the eightieth time he's suggested a classical-music storyline.

SHARON: You've had your classical music story this season.
Bobby Helpmann and the ballet?
You get one a year Berto, that's the rule.

BERT: It hasn't been shot yet and we've been trying to make that ep for—what—three seasons?

SHARON: All right … so it's Mozart's birthday …
Better be good.

BERT: And Molly knows how important Mozart's birthday is to Brendan—

SHARON: Picked Brendan as more of a Acker Dacker guy, but go on—

BERT: He's a male nurse. He's a sensitive soul. Of course he has a passion for Mozart. Which we'll start writing in now.

Brendan's been having a tough time at work. Things are feeling stale between him and Molly.

Molly decides the only way to fix it is to throw him a big party for Mozart's birthday.

Molly is beyond excited. She gets everyone doing delightful things for the party: Terence is manning the record player. Matron gives Brendan the afternoon off. Even Judy Loveday helps by making powidltascherl!

SHARON: What the strudel is powidltascherl?

BERT: Austrian plum jam turnovers—Mozart lived for them.

There's all of Mozart's greatest hits, every Austrian goodie you can think of, streamers, everyone he loves coming along to surprise him. Frank's dressed up as Mozart's Dad—he's been learning Figaro to present to them all. Even Bob's fired up to be learning about some new music.

Molly goes to pick up the piano cake—you know, like the one from *Women's Weekly*?

Beverley's made it for her and she goes to pick it up, and on the way home her car is hit by a drunk driver … or a fatigued driver.

SHARON: Bloody Beverley. Everything is her fault.

Lazy fucken bitch.

Would it be so hard to get off her bum and drop the *Women's Weekly* piano cake over to the Jones House?

BERT: She can't leave her house because she's the town's only phone operator. Even though it's 1985, but let's not worry about that—back to Molly—the car is hit! It spins across the road and ends up in a ditch.

We end ep one with her eyes staring out the window, not knowing if she's dead or not. The cake is a mess on the front seat.

Dun dun dun dun—

He's humming the A Country Practice *theme music which is what happens at the end of each ep.*

They're all thwacked by this.

SHARON: Oh mate!

I'm heartbroken!

I think the Mozart part is a fucken gooey wank, but I'm heartbroken here!

The drink driving thing is pretty genius too, because the Roads Authority and the CWA have been at us to do something about drink driving for a while.

This could work Berto, this could worko, Berto!

BERT: Then the next ep, we've got Brendan in the morgue identifying the body … the whole town falling apart … the guilt of the drink driver when he sobers up.

SHARON: Stories for days, mate, stories for days.

JUDY: It's affecting. It's really affecting.

DELL: It's heartbreaking.

JUDY: It's going to shock the audience. Devastate them.

They're all thinking it through.

JUDY: Is it too abrupt?
I can't help thinking the audience needs to be given time to say goodbye to Molly.

SHARON: It won't take long for some publicity prick at Seven to leak the news Annie's leaving, they'll know it's coming—

DELL: Maybe we need to use that?

JUDY: My instinct is that Molly needs to prepare everyone for her death.
Her friends in Wandin Valley and the audience.
She needs to help them realise that they'll be okay without her.
That's the person she is.
That's the show this is.

A beat.

If we're going to kill her, shouldn't we think about an illness?
It needs to be something we go through with her?
Something that, by the time she breathes her last, it's both monumentally heartbreaking, and also an incredible relief?
A death all of us dream of.

SHARON: You're a dark fucker, Jude.
You dream of your own death?

JUDY: Of course.

SHARON: And what's that?

JUDY: At home. With Barry, Luke and Chloe.

SHARON: And traumatise them for life?

JUDY: I was with my mum when she died.
There was a beauty to it.

SHARON: 'A beauty'?
See.
Only a dark fucker can think watching someone die has 'a beauty to it'.

JUDY: It's life. The cycle of life. The only thing we know for sure.
I'm glad I was there with Mum.

SHARON: Every death I've seen has been some poor bastard not going gently into the night.

BERT: At the end of a shiv while the guards weren't looking, Shaz?

Smashed up by a hot iron in the laundry room?

Brevilled as breakfast is being cooked?

SHARON: No-one wants to death-rattle their last in a Women's Correctional Facility, Bert.

JUDY: I think we need the actual death to be gentle, even if the lead-up isn't.

SHARON: I know you don't have your fatal cheat sheet mate, but any ideas?

SALLY: AIDS is the biggest health crisis in my hospital, and no-one understands it.

SHARON: How would a young mum in Wandin Valley get a poof's disease?

No offence Dell.

DELL: There's nothing offensive about being a 'poof', Sharon, so why would I take offence?

SALLY: This is what I'm talking about.

No-one knows anything about it but gossip and bullshit they get from tabloids and terrible television.

It's not just a disease for homosexual men.

Even if it was, we should be doing more about it, but it's not, and we could have the chance to really educate Australians about it.

BERT: How's your boy doing Dell?

DELL: He's okay.

His friends aren't.

But he's alright.

For now.

SHARON: In what world would Molly have AIDS?

SALLY: We know now that HIV—Human Immunodeficiency Virus—is carried from human to human by semen and blood.

So, sexual contact with a man who's infected, is one way.

SHARON: Brendan's not a poof.

We've worked hard to show a male nurse who's not a poof.

SALLY: Shaz, there's the blood thing too.

More women are becoming infected with the virus through sharing needles and blood transfusions.

SHARON: I don't buy Molly suddenly becoming a smacky who shares needles.

She's wacky but she's not a smacky.

SALLY: There are loads of reasons she could need a blood transfusion—losing blood in a car accident … or in a surgery … or pregnancy loss.

She could also be a haemophiliac … have severe anaemia?

Most of those ways would be completely realistic ways for someone like Molly to contract HIV, and ultimately full-blown AIDS.

SHARON: It's dark, Sally.

DELL: Good luck finding a disease to kill of a thirty-year-old that isn't dark Shaz.

SALLY: I hate seeing what these young blokes at work are going through.

Their own families are too scared to go near them.

Some cleaners won't go near their wards.

Some doctors won't.

It's bad.

If we killed Molly with AIDS, we could actually change all of that.

SHARON: We could also lose half the punters?

SALLY: Or we could bring that half around and make things easier for these boys.

DELL: What makes you think we'll lose half the punters?

SHARON: Because the whole country is fucken shit scared of it mate. And most people who live beyond fucken Surry Hills have never met a homo person.

JUDY: Of course they have—

DELL: We've got data on how powerful our *Mates* episodes were on exactly this—

SHARON: What does a death of AIDS look like, Sally?

SALLY: It's tough.

There's extreme weight loss. There can be diarrhoea. Fungal infections in the mouth and throat which make it very difficult to speak or eat. There are lesions that develop inside the mouth and on the skin—

SHARON: It's too dark mate.

DELL: It's important.

SHARON: 'Seven-thirty on a Monday night' stuff with the kids out of their baths, in their jammies, watching with their mum and dad?
Too fucken dark for that.
Do any of you want to watch her die like that? I don't.

DELL: We could make it so much better for these boys. We could change lives.

DELL *leaves the room.*

JUDY *goes after her.*

SHARON: Why don't we take a bit of a break?
Get some sugars and some coffees and some ciggies into us?

They do so. SALLY *continues at the table going through her notes.*

SALLY: It's important Shaz.
We need to do something on the show about it.
We'd make a big difference. I know it.

SHARON: It's not the time. Molly isn't the character.
Have a rattle around for some others, would ya?

Coffee is made. Lollies are eaten. Ciggies are lit up.

Enter JUDY.

BERT: Is she okay?

JUDY: We have to remember what's going on for her.

BERT: She's made of steel.

JUDY: She'll write a beautiful play about it all one day. We're so lucky.

BERT: Lucky, how?

JUDY: We actually are able to get stuff from our pain.

BERT: What do you mean?

JUDY: You know—all the stuff of our lives that hurts, or is confusing—we can put it into our work.

BERT: I've never really been that sort of writer.

JUDY: How do you work through anything painful if you can't write about it?

BERT: Mozart. A wander through the bush. A glass of Drambuie.

JUDY: Maybe you're the first writer in history who's not a mental case?

BERT: I write gags to come out of the mouths of people much funnier than me. I see my job as a very amusing kind of a jigsaw puzzle—

it's about getting to know the person and what makes them funny, and then figuring out which combination of words fit together to make the right laugh for them. For Cookie it's about a string of vaudevillian words full of bluster, for Esme, it's two or three suspicious words and some eyebrow work.

It's more physical and mathematical for me, not emotional.

JUDY: Oh god, Bert. Your parents loved you, didn't they?

BERT: I confess: adored me.

Enter DELL. SHARON *gives her a coffee and a biscuit.*

SHARON: We all right to go on, mates?

They are.

Dell? Mate?

When the time comes for us to do AIDS, and it will come, I'll make sure you're in the room.

If you want to be.

SHARON: What else have you got Sal?

SALLY: Oh! There's one I've been saving up for just the right person.

Hang on.

It's one of those jerks of an illness that is really easily missed in adults, thwacks them when they discover it and there's a slight chance of them beating it, but not much.

Also—it's more common in children, and children are more likely to live through it. For adults, because it's usually picked up late in the game, it's mostly curtains.

SHARON: We live for curtains.

SALLY: I've nursed a bunch of people with it over the years and only a few have survived it.

Oh! And, the treatment for adults is bloody awful.

SHARON: Don't tease us Sal, what is it?!

SALLY: Acute Lymphoblastic Leukaemia.

SHARON: Sounds sexy. Say it again?

SALLY: Acute Lymphoblastic Leukaemia.

SHARON: I mean, I'm wanting to root it already. Without a franga.

Tell me more about my new lover Sal.

SALLY: It'll do what we need.

Its initial symptoms overlap with—you know—being a woman.

Fatigue. Bleeding gums. Maybe a lump or two under the arms.

All the things that happen to us when we have bad periods, get pregnant or are generally exhausted from work and life.

Easy to dismiss as going too hard in life and needing a rest.

BERT: Which is easy with Molly, because she goes hard and definitely needs a rest.

SALLY: Exactly.

DELL: Imagine if Terence finds it too late?

Good story for him too—the guilt of not finding it early enough in her.

SHARON: Love it—

Am already seeing those Logie-winning scenes!

What's the chance of it turning around if Annie decides she wants to stay?

SALLY: We can do it.

It'd mean some pretty rotten treatment, but we could save her. Also, there are some interesting things being done with bone marrow transplants—we could get her in on a clinical trial or something.

Have Bob or someone donate their bone marrow?

BERT: Have Bob think that means losing actual bones—

SHARON: Give us the lifespan of this Leukaemia, Sal.

SALLY: Would you believe it's exactly fourteen weeks?

SHARON: You're fucken kidding.

SALLY: Of course I'm kidding.

BERT: Well done, Sally, another joke!

SHARON: Sally might just be as dark a bastard as Jude!

SALLY: That's the best compliment you've ever given me Shaz.

Lifespan of this leukaemia: she'd be tired. She'd be getting sick easily—you know, picking up every cold of Chloe's. Every cough Brendan comes home with. She'd maybe have a nosebleed now and then.

DELL: She's not going to bother Terence with those symptoms.

JUDY: She's going to have a sleep. Soldier on.

DELL: Put two teaspoons of international roast in her morning coffee, rather than one.

SHARON: Fucken welcome to being a woman.

SALLY: Exactly.

SHARON: She could even think she was preggers with all that shit, couldn't she? Get the punters thinking she's having that replacement Jones baby they've been jonesing for?

SALLY: For sure Shaz. But then … It's when she starts getting sore bones and a little short of breath Brendan thinks there might be something wrong. Lumps start to appear.

DELL: Then Terence is doing some tests.

SALLY: For viruses to begin with. Then he'd be more worried about the lumps around her underarms and breasts—are they breast cancer? Some sort of lymphoma? This will slow down getting the leukaemia diagnosis.

See, we're not often looking for leukaemia in adults. That's why it gets people.

Finally we get her to Sydney for the big tests, and see she's sick. Really sick. It's through her body and her bones.

And we have two medical options, depending on Annie.

She decides she wants to stay after all, and she fights it hard, and survives. We're talking chemo, lumbar punctures, experimental treatment.

Or Molly sees the writing on the wall—

JUDY: And decides she doesn't want her final weeks and days in a hospital in pain.

She wants to be at home with Brendan and Chloe.

DELL: She shows us all what living is about.

JUDY: Love.

Being with those you love.

BERT: Sounds gentler.

SALLY: It's not gentle.

It's awful.

But most things can be calmer with the right pain medication.

In TV terms, it's a slow goodbye.

SHARON: It's perfect.

Don't you mates think so?

They do.

JUDY: Well done Sally.

DELL: Perfect.

BERT: So we're killing Molly.

DELL: We're killing Molly.

They all look to JUDY.

JUDY: I'm killing Molly.

A beat.

SHARON: Sally—you'll get a brief together for all the writers on these eps about the leukaemia.

Probably a good look for the show to talk to a bunch of people with it?

You reckon you could get that going?

SALLY: Yep. I'll get in touch with the Leukaemia Foundation, the Cancer Council—I'm sure they'll connect us with some support groups, survivors, families.

SHARON: Great—we'll need to get this right.

As for you three—go home, get game ready.

We'll get you everything you need to know about this Acute Lymphoblastic Leukaemia.

Read it all. Live your everyday life imagining the person you most love has it.

Berto?

BERT: Cancer jokes?

SHARON: Your best cancer jokes.

Dell, we'll be needing your best stoic, survivor, community working together porn.

Jude, sharpen those pencils, this is going to be your most beautiful slaying yet.

We'll meet in a couple of months to plot the deed.

PART TWO

A Country Practice *Story Room. Months later.*

Enter BERT. *He's crying.*

He switches on the lights. Before he begins to set up the room, he takes a cassette out of his satchel and puts it into the player. It's Mozart's 'Requiem in D Minor.' He cries harder.

He lights a cigarette and begins to set up the room. He goes in and out of the room collecting stuff for the tasks he has. Ciggie never leaves his mouth. Cries.

DELL *and* JUDY *enter together. Gives them both tearful hugs.*

JUDY: I thought I'd be the first to crack up.

BERT *goes to say something, can't, cries and leaves the room.*

DELL: How lucky is his Evelyn?

Thoroughly pleasant, likes going to the opera and cries over the death of a character in a tellie show.

I'll bet he even picks up his towel from the floor.

JUDY: I'll bet he doesn't.

Your episode was beautiful, Dell.

I took it down to the creek near home and read it.

DELL: Thanks darling.

JUDY: Really beautiful.

Loved the scene where they're all at the maternity window waving at her.

DELL: I cried all the way through writing it.

JUDY: I cried all the way through reading it.

DELL: I can't believe we're doing it. We're actually doing it.

JUDY: I'm a bit scared I won't pull it off.

DELL: Of course you will.

JUDY: It's everywhere.

DELL: I don't think I've picked up a newspaper or a magazine in a month that hasn't mentioned it!

JUDY: The ratings are up there with Vicki and Simon's wedding!

DELL: It's all anyone wants to talk to me about anywhere!

JUDY: I even had a reporter from the *Herald* finding *me* for the scoop.

DELL: My neighbour's running a book on whether she goes or we save her!

JUDY: And the feelings, Dello! The feelings!

DELL: So many feelings from so many strangers.

JUDY: Chloe's best friend is taking it really badly.

She was over for dinner the other night begging me to save her. Begging, Dell.

Snotty tears.

The works.

I've even been getting mail! To my house!

Addressed thus: 'The Lady Who Writes For *A Country Practice*' Post Office. Berry. New South Wales.

DELL: I got letters to the theatre, which of course I thought were fan letters about my profound partnership with Toni Lamond.

Nope. They were pleading for the life of Molly Jones.

JUDY: Have you ever seen anything like it?

DELL: Never.

The *Number Ninety-Six* bomb was pretty big—but not like this.

JUDY: How are things with your play?

DELL: La Lamond is taking it on the road.

JUDY: Brilliant!

DELL: Any poet news?

JUDY: Yes! I mean it's not Toni Lamond Is Touring My Play news, but it's news for a poet and we so rarely get news to share—

DELL: You poor poets.

JUDY: Yes, we poor poets.

DELL: We wheel you out for every important moment in our lives, but we leave you poor and having to teach primary school or write television drama—

JUDY: Guess who's had three poems put in next year's Sixth Form curriculum?!

DELL: JD Baxter?!

JUDY: JD Baxter!

DELL: Up your arse, Gwen Harwood!

JUDY: I love Gwen Harwood.

DELL: I love JD Baxter.

Up your arse, Les Murray!

JUDY: Well, I love Les too, but he's on enough school reading lists, so up your arse Les Murray!

DELL: Jude, this is wonderful. Which poems?

JUDY: 'Bush burning', 'I watched you shift your shape' and 'Mr Callum's night terrors'.

DELL: Interesting.

JUDY: That they're including 'night terrors'?

DELL: Yep.

JUDY: Apparently wanting to look at the history of ratbaggery and hoax in Australian poetry.

DELL: Jude it's wonderful!

May you inspire hordes of young punks to be poets and literary ratbags.

JUDY: Or hordes of young punks to roll their eyes whenever my name is mentioned as they recover from the worst year of their schooling life?

Bert! Why are we listening to this depressing music? It's making me want to impale myself on that box of pencils.

Exit BERT, *crying.*

Enter SHARON *with two postal bags full of letters that she proceeds to pour onto the table.*

SHARON: Kevin in the mail room told me if we don't hurry up and off Molly we'll have to carry him off to Callan Park—

They open some of the mail and read.

Anything threatening, give over here.

JUDY *hands over a letter. Opens another. Hands it over.*

JUDY: I thought our viewers were nice people.

SHARON: Not when we're 'murdering' their favourite character.

JUDY: Here's a nice one?

'Dear *ACP*, thank you for the sensitive way that you've treated Molly's illness. My sister died of leukaemia two years ago and it's been very comforting to our family to watch another family deal with those same things. We're desperately hoping Molly lives, so there's a happy ending for us, at least on our favourite television show. Yours, Margery Peters.'

Oh. Goodness!

DELL: 'Dear Cast and Crew of *A Country Practice*, please find enclosed this petition to save the life of Molly Jones. From the people of Wellington, NSW.'

She opens the letter out. It's very, very long.

SHARON: To add to petitions from the people of Tenterfield, New South Wales. Campbell Town, Tasmania. Port Lincoln, South Australia. Albany, Western Australia.

Enter BERT, *still crying.*

BERT: Palmerston, Northern Territory. Silverton, New South Wales.

DELL: Bert darling, can I get you a tea? A coffee?

SHARON: He needs a quaalude. You got a quaalude? A Valium? A spliff? Have any of you squares got a spliff?

Dell. Surely you have a spliff.

BERT: I'm right thanks.

JUDY: (Has he been like this all week?)

Berto. I didn't know you were so attached to her—

SHARON: It's not Molly.

Evelyn's gone back to America.

DELL: For a holiday? Bert?

Has Evelyn gone back to America for a holiday?

BERT: She's fallen in love with the Key Grip on *Crocodile Dundee*.

He's a former Australian Heavyweight Body Building Champion.

He's twenty-seven.

They're living in a 'loft conversion apartment' in the Meatpacking District of Manhattan.

She doesn't want to be married anymore.

JUDY: Oh, Bert!

DELL: Bert! You're living in a Woody Allen film!

When did this happen?

SHARON: Earlier this week.

DELL: Berto, darling, shouldn't you be taking time off?

SHARON: He can't take time off—we need jokes more than ever this week!

BERT: Aren't we killing her today?
What's possibly funny about it or anything else?
SHARON: Can we get this fucken song off?
No wonder you're a basket case, it's fucken depressing as shit mate.
BERT: It's Mozart's Requiem.
There couldn't be a more appropriate piece of music for what we're about to do.
For the tragedy of being a human soul trying to live this life!
SHARON: Mate.
You've got to pull yourself together.
We need you today.
DELL: Bert.
I didn't ever feel like you liked your wife all that much.
BERT: Of course I liked her. I loved her.
DELL: I'm not sure you did.
I think you did that classic small town boy from Australia thing: you had a root and fell in love.
You did, darling.
I'm sorry if you think that's crude, but that's exactly what happened.
She absolutely wasn't your sort of person.
BERT: Why are we talking about her in the past tense?
DELL: Because, darling, she is a past tense and you need to move on.
You're never getting her back from a twenty-seven-year-old key grip on a movie set—
A twenty-seven-year-old grip is a man of the body, and I bet he can fix things.
And Bert, you're a man of the mind, you can't fix things, can you?
BERT: Of course I can't fix things.
DELL: Exactly. You simply can't compete.
JUDY: Dell, it's only been a few days—
DELL: But has it, Bert?
Has it really?
She didn't ever want to do anything with you.
She didn't come to concerts.

She didn't come to plays.

And Bert, darling, you were perfectly happy with that.

BERT: I was?

DELL: You were.

Remember the grand time we had when my play opened?

BERT: It was a grand time.

DELL: Where was Evelyn?

BERT: At home.

DELL: And my question to you is: could you have had such a grand time if she was there?

BERT: I don't know that I would have.

DELL: Then stop your crying and realise that you've been given a gift!

Someone leaving you, who you don't much like anyway, it's a freedom!

You'll come with me to the Marble Bar tonight after work, we'll drink cocktails and we'll plan the next week of concerts and plays and bars and fun, all right?

BERT: Fun?

DELL: Yes Bert.

That's what being a divorcee is.

It's very, very fun. Kids are grown up. Spare cash for a martini or five.

Being single is an absolute hoot!

Enter SALLY, *who's visibly pregnant. Laden down with medical books.* JUDY *helps her.*

Look at this vision. Bringing life into the world.

She's set to have absolutely no fun for the next eighteen years.

Not us, Berto!

SALLY: It's impossible to say 'Good morning' today, don't you think?

When we're set to do what we're going to do?

Are we really going to do it?

SHARON: We're really going to do it.

JUDY: No final stays of execution?

SHARON: Ah, let's see where Dell's beautiful episode left us.

DELL: Thank you, Shaz.

They each pull out a script and read at the end.

SHARON: 'Brendan, will you give me three wishes?'
ALL: 'Take off the mask, kiss me, take me home.'
SHARON: There's never been a suicide more poetic on Australian TV.
SALLY: Suicide? We haven't talked about suicide or euthanasia or—
I haven't got anything prepared—
SHARON: Mate. Calm your farm.
JUDY: It's a metaphorical suicide.
She was in the hospital because she's so vulnerable she can't even risk a kiss from Chloe.
It's no way to live if you don't have much time left.
SHARON: Taking off the mask, having a pash, going home—
JUDY: Molly's decided to die.
SHARON: Righto.
Has everyone had their coffee? A ciggie? A lolly?
Have we all caught up on the latest?
Has everyone tried to light a firecracker up Bert's arse?
Let's do this.

They gather at the table. They're reticent to sit down. When they sit down, they have to kill Molly.

I wonder if this is how Mark Antony and his mates felt when they gathered to plan the execution of Julius Caesar?
Or that poor bastard who had to cut off the head of them queens Henry the Eighth didn't want anymore?
Or—
SALLY: Aren't we more the palliative team who are deciding there won't be any more treatment?
SHARON: Clean it up how you like, mate.
Today there's a hit put out on TV's favourite mother, wife and caretaker of Doris the Pig: Molly Jones.
JUDY: And, as ever, my name will be on the opening titles for all to see.
SHARON: No-one bumps off an innocent like you Jude.
DELL: You don't have three 'Golden Teardrop' awards for nothing, Jude.
JUDY: Which locations do we have? What's cast availability? What do we need to juggle?
SHARON: Blank chequebook, mate.
JUDY: What?!

SHARON: We can have whoever we want, whenever we want them.

Hell—we can shoot it on Sydney Harbour Bridge at peak hour, if we found a reason to slay Molly there.

All main cast and supporting cast are booked for the entire week.

Jim says whatever we dream up, we can have.

JUDY: Wow!

We didn't even get that for Vicki and Simon's wedding!

SHARON: No B and C storylines.

All Molly.

BERT: Molly drowning in a bath of Dom Perignon?

DELL: He's back!

He's not. The tears start again.

SHARON: Jim reckons instead of the B and C storylines, we put in flashbacks of some of Molly's funnier moments, so it's not an absolute festival of depresso for the whole hour.

DELL: Flashbacks—

SHARON: Boss wants them.

DELL: —are hideous.

SHARON: They'll pep things up.

BERT: Make the punters cry for the old Molly.

DELL: Too sentimental.

SHARON: Dell we're a soap on a commercial network.

DELL: We're not a soap.

SHARON: Fancy Playwright Dell forgets we're not all high art and bloody subtext.

Some of us just want a car chase, a romance and a bit of a cry.

DELL: This show is more than that.

SHARON: Is it?

DELL: We're a drama series about truthful relationships and what's going on in our society.

SHARON: With a wombat called Fatso and a pig called Doris?

And a living muppet at the club called Cookie?

JUDY: We're all those things.

BERT: That's why we rate.

JUDY: We're soap.

BERT: We're sitcom.

JUDY: We're medical drama.

DELL: We're social commentary.

And we're better than flashbacks in what's most likely going to be our most watched episode ever.

SHARON: We're not mate, because ultimately the name at the top of the show is Jim Davern's, and the boss has the horn for a flashback.

So the ep has flashbacks.

Righto—who's in the show and what do we need from them?

She's at the butchers paper.

From Molly—we need to see her last breath, of course, but—

JUDY: We need to see she's made peace with dying.

We need to see she thinks Brendan and Chloe will be okay.

SHARON: Sally, where are we at with the illness?

SALLY: She's highly immunocompromised.

And, she's coming home to a farm—a germ festival. Animals and the dirt associated with them are terrible for a sick person.

She's really sick. And she can get even sicker, and fast.

SHARON: How long have we got her?

SALLY: Anything from a day or two to a few weeks. Even longer. Bodies are amazing. The way people fight to stay alive never ceases to amaze me. They fight hard.

JUDY: And Molly would fight hard.

DELL: But is she still fighting hard?

SHARON: Let's make it a day or two. We don't need this episode running over weeks, especially without any B or C plots.

JUDY: And how can we see her get weaker?

SHARON: Can we do it without spewing or bleeding or any bullshit like that?

SALLY: Of course.

Terence and Brendan can feed her more painkillers.

It can be peaceful.

SHARON: Because 'peaceful' makes dazzling drama, mates.

JUDY: I can get drama in 'peaceful'. So can these actors.

DELL: They've been extraordinary.

SHARON: They've been fucken spectacular.

JUDY: The work they've been doing.

Molly, Brendan, Simon, Vicki, Bob!

Bob's been breaking my heart!

SHARON: And Terence—fuck me, did you see his face when he sent her to Sydney for the tests?

DELL: Shane Porteous.

He's a matinee idol.

JUDY: Is he Dell, or is he just tall, with a full head of hair?

DELL: Luscious, silvering, substantial hair.

SHARON: Dell and her warms for Dr Terence …

DELL: I fully admit it. I adore the man. He wakes up parts of my body I didn't know existed.

There's a reason I get all the episodes where he has a romance, or a romance gone wrong, or a creepy middle-aged stalker—

SHARON: Because you're his creepy middle-aged stalker?

DELL: 'Middle-aged'?

Darling, thank you. I love you.

And yes. I live to be his creepy middle-aged stalker.

You know I've made a pass at him at the last three Logies.

BERT: You did? What did he say?

DELL: Oh he's darling. Every year.

Just like Terence. 'Dell, I'm very flattered, but I'm afraid I'm very happily married.'

BERT: And what do you say to that?

DELL: I said 'Darling, we're at the Logies in Melbourne. Your wife is in the Blue Mountains. You're the star of the country's biggest television show and you need to start behaving like it.'

BERT: Ha!

That would have brought him around?

DELL: Sadly, no.

BERT: How could he say no?

DELL: I'll try again this year.

One year I'll break him.

He won't know himself.

SHARON: Let's keep moving.

I want us to have the ep plotted today so Judy can go and start writing it tomorrow. We've got a reading with the actors next week.

Brendan?

JUDY: There's going to be a real tension for him—between his own pain and showing Molly she doesn't have to worry about him after—

BERT: Do we need to seed a new romance from Brendan?

ALL: NO!

SHARON: Vicki?

DELL: Vicki is pregnant with the twins. Her hormones are all over the place so I think we have an opportunity to let her be emotional for once.

She's bringing new life into the world, while Molly's life is ending.

Just looking at Vicki and her belly is to look at hope.

She's desperate to talk to Molly about Chloe's future. About a pull she's having towards being able to mother Chloe. But because she's famously completely uptight, she can't.

Does Vicki spend Molly's last days avoiding her?

BERT: That's awful.

DELL: It's also true to her character. Vicki comes to everything later than she should.

She's got all sorts of walls up—and sometimes when people have walls up, it's because they're emotionally very scared and unable to be vulnerable.

Isn't that right, Shaz?

SHARON: I'll remind you, old dame, I'm your fucken boss.

But, yeah bloody oath.

DELL: We've then got the drama of whether Vicki will say what she needs to say before Molly dies?

Or will she live in regret at not having been brave enough to be real with her best friend?

SHARON: And what do you think she does Dello?

DELL: For story purposes, I'd love it that she doesn't make it.

For Vicki, I want her to have the closure.

JUDY: Feels to me like it's an episode of closure and emotions.

What do we want the audience to take from this story? This episode?

They all think on it.

It's important to love, speak that love, make sure your person knows she's loved.

SHARON: Then let's get them together for a tear-jerker scene about mothering.
Simon?

BERT: Simon is there to support Brendan and Vicki. He's a carer. It's subtle.

SHARON: How about Dell's boyfriend Penis Porteous?

DELL: There's a new woman in town, a glorious playwright with—

DELL *describes how she looks.*

Terence is devastated. He's guilt-ridden. He's questioning his life in medicine—if he can't save this bright spark, what's the point?

SHARON: Does he get on the turps?

DELL: No.

JUDY: We see all the guilt, but not any boozing. It's not about him.
Let's just see him being sad.

DELL: And lovely?
With a scene of him getting out of the shower, dressing and being sad and lovely?
The man has to clean himself.
You know the man loves to clean himself.

SHARON: I think we should give Judy Loveday a good scene.
She's been nursing her.

JUDY: Judy Loveday is losing one of the only people in Wandin Valley who actually likes her.

SALLY: Why are you always so cruel to Judy Loveday?

JUDY: She's a meanie.

DELL: She doesn't suffer fools.

JUDY: Let's use the whole glass-half-empty vibe she has to voice what we're all thinking: why does Molly have to die, while some grumpy old bastard lives another day in the Muldoon Wing to throw his roast dinner at his nurses?

SHARON: Perfect. Life is fucked, isn't it?
How many ninety-year-old windbags do you know sucking up oxygen when some poor twenty-year-old with everything to live for gets taken down with some shitful disease?

BERT: We also need to give old Bob Hatfield a scene.

JUDY: Bob loves Molly.

BERT: He's loved her since her first episode.

SHARON: And not in a Dell loves Dr Terence in the shower way.

BERT: In a gentle, appropriate way. It's a big loss for him.
He's worked hard on keeping the farm going while she's been sick.
Let's give him some time with her?

SHARON: Fine by me.
Let's get everyone else together somehow—like that beautiful scene at the window you did, Dell. Genius.

JUDY: Do we start the episode with her funeral?

DELL: And *flashback* to the days leading up?

SHARON: We've got enough flashbacks already, mate.

SALLY: What if she has a funeral while she's alive?
Molly seems like someone who'd love to see her own funeral?
I had a patient with one a few weeks back.

SHARON: What the fuck? Someone alive for their own funeral?
Sounds like a massive fucken drag.

SALLY: It was the opposite!
I went away thinking everyone should be at their own funeral!
The future dead person gets to hear all the great things people think about them.

JUDY: Is it in a church?

SALLY: The one I went to was in a school of arts.
Was all decked out with pictures of the future dead person—

SHARON: Did this future dead person have a name? So we can stop calling them 'Future Dead Person'?

SALLY: Her name was Cathy.

SHARON: 'Was' Cathy? She's dead now?

SALLY: Yeah she died a few days after. After her funeral. That she went to.

SHARON: What happened?

SALLY: It was like a normal funeral.
Instead of bringing in in a coffin, her daughters pushed her in her wheelchair to her favourite music.
She sat at the front as this procession of people who loved her got up and delivered eulogies. Her grandson talked about how when his number came up for Vietnam, she taught him how to roll the most perfect spliffs … and then he taught the congregation how to roll the most perfect spliffs!

Her best friend remembered the time Cathy poisoned their handsie boss at the RSL by making a chocolate mudcake packed with laxatives. And there was a little container of Ford Pills under a bunch of seats—like lucky door prizes!

Her husband got up, cried before he started talking and said he'd miss making her tea in the morning. He'd miss fighting about Malcolm Fraser and Gough. He'd miss her soft hands and her hard slap on the bum when he got home from bowls.

I can't believe this is making me cry! For god's sake. Sorry. I'm all over the place.

And then—and then—

Cathy's daughter brought the microphone to her and she said all the things she needed to say. That she loved her girls and her grandkids and her husband. That she hadn't forgotten what Cecily Taylor did to her and if she can haunt anyone she'll haunt that rotten bitch. That as much as she loved her family, her best friend Addie was the absolute love of her life and the person she'll miss the most and try to find a way to haunt lovingly.

It was just the best show I've ever been to.

SHARON: I love it.

JUDY's crying too.

Let's do it with Molly. Except we won't have her coming out as having a boner for Vicki.

SALLY: Why would Molly have a boner for Vicki?

SHARON: The love of Cathy's life being her best friend?

DELL: Don't you have a best friend Shaz?

SHARON: Of course I have a best friend.
Valmay Johnson.
Met pulling apart a scrag fight on my second day in the slammer.
Been besties ever since.

DELL: Is there a man in the world who's been better to you?
Who you've loved more than Valmay Johnson?

SHARON: Of course not.

DELL: Love of life, see?

SHARON: Val loves dick.

JUDY: Okay. Back to Molly's funeral.

SHARON: Let's get plotting.

I reckon final scene is Molly dying.

It's after the joy of funeral where she's alive—the penultimate.

She writes these on the board in the places for the last two scenes.

A beat.

JUDY: How old was this Cathy, Sally?

SALLY: Seventy-nine.

JUDY: She'd been sick for a while?

SALLY: Cardiomyopathy.

Had somehow stayed ahead of it for about ten years, until she couldn't anymore.

JUDY: A long life, and well lived, by the sound of things.

SALLY: Definitely Judy. She was terrific.

Even when she was hooked up to the oxygen machine with monitors all over her, there was a spirit.

An undiminished spirit.

Like Molly.

BERT: And as history's greatest writer of television before us said—'Aye, there's the rub'.

DELL: Molly's death is a tragedy.

JUDY: There's a toddler she won't see grow up.

DELL: There's so much left undone.

JUDY: So much potential.

DELL: So much love.

JUDY: Taken.

DELL: Being at your own funeral is fine for old bastards like us, but for young bastards like Molly?

JUDY: Or someone like you, Sally, with twins on the way and a whole life ahead?

The tragedy of it outweighs the celebration of the short life.

SHARON: But imagine it, mates.

Molly being wheeled down the aisle by Brendan, Chloe on her lap.

DELL: It's too sad, love.

SHARON: We're all about the sad, mate.

JUDY: Way too sad.

BERT: Why not have a barbecue?

SHARON: Biggest episode of the year and you want to shoot Frank flipping sausages and blagging on about the superiority of his homemade tomato sauce?

BERT: There isn't a problem on this earth that can't be fixed with a barbie—

SHARON: Or throwing a 'shrimp' on one, eh, Bert?

BERT *cries again.*

JUDY: Too soon, Shaz!

DELL: A barbecue is perfect.

JUDY: We get everyone there, she's surrounded by love.

BERT: Cookie and Bob can burn something! Or bring a special sauce they're planning to sell to every house in Australia!

SHARON: Then we kill her?

A beat.

JUDY: Then we kill her.

SHARON: Let's plot.

They sit down.

SHARON *chucks* JUDY *a box of tissues and grabs the cards she's going to pop on the cork board.*

She writes 'flashback' on a bunch and sticks them up at regular intervals.

With each new idea, she scribbles a number and a word or two— eg '1. Brendan, home, prepping.' '2. Judy gets Molly ready, hospital.' Filling up the empty spaces for scenes.

JUDY: Let's start at Jones House with Brendan, alone.
For a moment it might look like he's already widowed.
He's not.
He's preparing the house for Molly to come home.

DELL: Nice, Jude.

SHARON: How's he feeling?
Is he letting some emotion go?

JUDY: Not yet.
He's trying to get on with things.

SHARON: Righto.

Then back to the hospital where Judy Loveday is helping Molly go home.

JUDY: She's being kind for once in her life?

DELL: Jude …

We can see she's terribly upset, but she's doing everything she can to help Molly.

Judy Loveday being Judy Loveday though, we can't help but see how scared she is for Molly.

JUDY: Judy's self esteem isn't great. She's thinking—why her and not me? Why Molly, who has everything?

Is that the truth of what's happening for her?

SHARON: Good luck putting that in the big print, Jude.

BERT: Do we go back the Jones House and Brendan?

Simon's helping him dress Chloe? This could be funny. Mixing up buttons?

SHARON: I reckon we need to get to Vicki.

I know we don't officially have our usual B and C plots, but really, Vicki's teeny tiny small fucken balls, that's our B plot.

Terence's guilt, that's our C plot.

DELL: Vicki's balls are perfectly sized.

She just doesn't know what to say to Molly.

SHARON: Bowen House it is. Simon and Vicki.

They're about to lose their best friend, half a second before they have twins.

DELL: We need to set it up early, from Vicki, the real reason she's avoiding Molly.

You'll need to spell it out, Jude, no subtext.

Otherwise the audience will spend the whole episode furious at Vicki rather than loving Molly.

SHARON: It goes there.

'How do I talk to her about life after she's not here?' or something like that.

How do we think Simon will take this?

If it was the other way around, she'd be telling him to pull it together.

Does he do that?

BERT: He gives her time.
Knows it's hard for her.

SHARON: From Bowen House, let's get outdoors.
Brendan's driving Molly up the driveway home—maybe for the last time.

JUDY: She's relieved.

DELL: She's there with her people and her animals.

JUDY: She's home.

BERT: She's seeing the town have all been there, painting the place bright colours.

JUDY: Can't believe the community cares about her so much.

SHARON: Of course they fucken do.

JUDY: We've got to get to the barbecue from here.
Is it happening on this day?

SHARON: Nah, too much.

JUDY: Then it's about the day-to-day stuff?
Seeing them have their tea?
Playing with Chloe?

SHARON: Scintillating TV, mate.

JUDY: It will be because she's doing these things for the last time.
She's having day-to-day moments with people she loves.
Just thinking … I reckon we move the barbecue up.
If it's the penultimate, we lose that emotional stuff from Vicki and Terence.

DELL: Jude's right. If the B and C stories are Vicki and Terence, best they're resolved closer to the end of the episode than the barbecue.

BERT: Let's have Bob visit.

DELL: He needs to be doing something tender we wouldn't normally see.

JUDY: That we'd only see him do with Molly.

DELL: Blowing up balloons with Chloe?
Keeping them all distracted?

JUDY: Beautiful.
Big, awkward, gallumping Bob, on the floor, blowing up pink balloons with Chloe.
Doing anything he can to be around Molly before she dies.
And she's getting weaker.

SHARON: You can't help it can you, mate?

Killing her softly—

DELL: Let's signpost the barbecue next.

BERT: At the Club—have Shirley and Esme talking about the barbecue.

DELL: Let's get some Esme fret in there: Are they imposing? Should they really be taking time away from this young couple?

JUDY: The whole town is sad.

DELL: Especially Terence.

BERT: Do we want someone, maybe Esme, saying something to Terence about not finding the cancer earlier?

DELL: She wouldn't.

SHARON: She might.

ALL: NO!

DELL: Shaz, my feeling is the drama in this ep is coming from our characters being sensitive and kind to each other.

Anything else would just be too painful.

JUDY: This is a kind death.

SHARON: Let's get back to Jones House from The Club.

DELL: Terence in front of Molly.

Let's give that silver fox some big, juicy, tender feelings.

JUDY: Easy tiger.

He needs to go over to check on her.

Make sure she's comfortable.

Results of the latest tests and such. Painkillers?

SHARON: Sal—what might he have?

SALLY: The epicillin, the antibiotic he's got her on, doesn't seem to be working? She's got pneumonia, and the beginnings of petechial spots—

JUDY: How do you spell that?

SALLY: P-E-T-E-C-H-I-A-L—they're little haemorrhages.

She'd be starting to cough more too with the pneumonia.

Her lungs are filling up with fluid.

It's getting harder for her.

By this stage we'd be looking at some pretty heavy-duty painkillers.

Maybe even morphine.

SHARON: I don't think we'd need the detail—'something for your pain' is enough.

What's Terence feeling and thinking?
Let's see it all.
He knows it's the fucken pointy end.

JUDY: Let's get Chloe into this scene.

SHARON: What's she doing?

DELL: Something ordinary.
Something everyday.
She's playing with her dolls.
Oblivious that she's living through the life event that will define her.

JUDY: Perfect.

SHARON: Fucken breaks Terence's heart.

JUDY: He kisses Molly. Tells her he loves her.

SHARON: Not in a 'Dell loves my schlong' kinda way, in a genuine way.

DELL: True friendship.

JUDY: And then comes the barbecue. Perfect spot.

BERT: We need Cookie to burn his hand or something to give us a bit of a breather from how we're getting closer to losing Molly.

SHARON: You know they'll be looking at their clocks at home—

JUDY: Let's set her up on a lovely, long couch, where she can see everyone.

SHARON: Doing the sums on how long it is till eight-thirty—

DELL: Like a queen at court.

JUDY: Here, you big sook.

SHARON: Counting down until the execution.
What shenanigans can we have at the grill, Bert?

BERT: Esme's so sad she decides she'll drink a beer.
Bob and Cookie fight about the best way to cook a sausage.
Frank's blagging on about having marinated the steak—

SHARON: Which Bob and Cookie will think is a waste of perfectly good steak. Because it is.

BERT: We all know the only thing worth putting near a steak is a tomato sauce!

SHARON: Shit I feel better already.
Vicki's still being a soft cock and avoiding Molly.

DELL: Simon sits with Molly.
Together, they watch Vicki avoiding Molly—they talk about it.

Molly understands.

She'll get there, Simon tells her.

JUDY: Let's have him say something particularly grown up so Molly can tell him he'll make a great father?

That's her one-on-one goodbye to him.

DELL: She's right!

JUDY: She is.

He will make a good father!

SHARON: Don't you start.

We're finished if you start.

DELL: It's just so sad. For all of them.

JUDY: For Molly too!

Can you imagine lying on a couch, watching what life will be like when you're not there anymore?

There's Brendan having a beer with Judy Loveday.

There's Chloe playing with a new toy.

Life will go on without her and here's what it's going to look like.

SHARON: And that's the end of the barbie.

Close on Chloe being oblivious to it all. Loving her new toy.

Secondlast ad break.

They all grab some tissues.

Nighttime at Jones House? Is it their last night?

JUDY: Can they have one more day together?

DELL: Let's give them one more day?

SHARON: Okay you fucken sappy bastards. Their second last night together.

JUDY: Molly says they need to talk about life after she's gone.

He can't.

BERT: He doesn't want there to be a time when she's not there.

JUDY: In that case then, she'll talk for him.

She doesn't want him to be lonely.

She wants him to move on.

There will come a time when he'll meet someone and he mustn't feel guilty about that.

He's got to go for it.

BERT: But he has to promise her one thing.

SALLY: Oh, god, what?!

BERT: That he won't marry Beverley.

They all laugh.

SHARON: Poor fucken Beverley.

DELL: I'd like to propose, Shaz, as a reward for going through three and a half months of Molly dying, that we give them a real life Beverley.

That she's an actual body with an actual storyline, and she's actually a bombshell like Helen Morse?

SHARON: Not on my watch.

BERT: Beverley is forever the silent telephone operator until Wandin Valley gets with the times and has Telecom install proper phone lines.

SHARON: And she has the thickest ankles and the frizziest hair in the southern hemisphere. And she smells like a mouldy egg sandwich that's been in your kid's lunchbox since the first day of term. Helen Morse she is not.

BERT: How do you know Brendan's not partial to a thick ankle?

I know plenty of men partial to a thick ankle.

I, for one, love a thick ankle. Sturdy!

SHARON: Anyone want a break?

Or will we push on with the tough stuff while Bert's mooning on about thick ankles?

This is a good spot to wrap up Terence's storyline.

DELL: Back to Jones House for another check?

SHARON: I don't think there's anything new with that.

SALLY: Her vital signs are deteriorating?

It's getting closer to curtains?

SHARON: I think Terence is in the surgery on the turps after all.

JUDY: It's not right that he's drunk this close to the end.

SHARON: What if he's not drunk, but he and Simon are at the surgery having a drink, talking it through?

DELL: Terence upset he couldn't save her.

JUDY: Upset that you can't heal everyone.

DELL: Upset at himself for getting too close to a patient.

Doctor stuff.

SHARON: It's *A Country Practice* for fuck's sake.

JUDY: I think we go back to Molly and Brendan now and we stay there until the end.

DELL: Molly and Vicki need to make peace.

BERT: You know someone's definitely dying because Simon and Brendan offer to do the washing up—

DELL: Which leaves Molly and Vicki to go to the lounge room.

JUDY: Molly's so weak, Vicki has to help her.

DELL: They sit together and it all comes spilling out of Vicki.

Chloe's going to need a woman around and Vicki wants Molly to know she can be that woman if she wants her to be.

She'll do anything Molly wants.

Anything Molly needs.

JUDY: Molly needs Vicki to tell her about Molly—all the good stuff. Who she is, what she cared about, what sort of mother she was, what sort of friend she was.

Not this sad stuff at the end, but everything else.

Can Vicki promise to do that?

DELL: She can. They hug.

JUDY: A hug that uses everything Molly has left.

SHARON: Final ad break.

SHARON *gets up and goes to her bag.*

Gets out a bottle of scotch. Goes out to the hall and brings back five glasses.

Pours them all with the scotch.

Home stretch.

To Molly!

ALL: To Molly.

They all drink. SALLY *drinks and spits hers back into the glass.*

SHARON: It's a new day at Jones House.

JUDY: Molly and Chloe are making wind chimes or sticking photos in an album or something.

SHARON: It's a fucken lovely time.

JUDY: That night, we see Brendan and Molly in bed together.

Brendan can't sleep.

BERT: Poor Brendan.

JUDY: He goes downstairs to get a drink and finds a scrapbook Molly's been making for Chloe.

It's the most beautiful, colourful, homemade version of the life they've had together.

It's pure Molly. In her voice over, we hear about when they met … we hear about them coming to Wandin Valley … we hear about them having Chloe … we hear about them losing Christopher.

There's one scene left on the board.

The mood is sombre.

SHARON: Jude. You know her the best. You're writing the episode.
How do you think she'd want to die?

JUDY: On the farm with Brendan and Chloe.

SHARON: We've got her there.

JUDY: I think she'd want to be outside, don't you?

SHARON: You know better than any of us, Jude—

JUDY: I think she'd—
I think we need wind chimes.
She needs to be somewhere where we can hear the wind chimes?
On the couch like at the barbecue?
Brendan and Chloe just going about their day, picking flowers or collecting the eggs and—

SHARON: I don't think that's quite it, mate.
We're close.
We're not there yet.
Fuck me I like the idea of wind chimes haunting Australia's dreams for the next few months though, that's a top idea Jude.

JUDY: No! I've got it!
Go back. Scene Sixteen. We've got Bob and Molly blowing up pink balloons, haven't we?
Scrap the balloons.
They're carefully, lovingly stitching a kite.
It's for Chloe, for after she's gone.
The last beautiful thing Molly makes.

DELL: Something to fly high, and wave from above.
Perfect.

JUDY: Back to our end scene.
How about this?
Brendan's dragged the couch out to one of the bigger paddocks.
The paddock: it's lush and green.
The grass is long and it's swaying in the breeze.
Molly is propped up on the couch from the barbecue—all rugged up. Dressed in something bright. Fun earrings. Pure Molly, if she wasn't so sick. Snug as a bug in a rug.
She's watching Brendan teach Chloe how to fly the kite we've just seen her so carefully making.
She's watching from some distance.
He waves at her. A 'Look at our little girl, isn't she wonderful?' wave.
They smile at each other.
Close in on Molly's face smiling.
Then back to Brendan.

She thinks for a moment. They're all on tenterhooks.

He sees something's off and starts running towards her—
The screen goes to black as though it's her eyes closing.
And through that darkness we hear Brendan shout. It's distraught, almost primal.
He shouts 'Molly!'
And the credits roll.
[*Humming the theme song*] Dun dun dun dun.

They're all howling.

They've cracked the back of this story.

They know they've done it. There are hugs and tears and drinking.

SHARON: You did it Jude.
They don't call you TV's Most Wanted Serial Killer for nothing.
JUDY: What can I say? I've been blessed. I can do a good death.
SHARON: Fucken Kleenex better get cutting down more trees because tissue demand is about to head through the roof.
WE MADE SOME TEE VEE TODAY
Sing with me mates!

They do.

ALL: WE MADE SOME TEE VEE TODAY
WE'LL GET THOSE RATINGS SKY HIGH
WE'LL MAKE THE PUNTERS ALL CRY
WE MADE SOME TEE VEE TODAY
MY MATES!

SHARON: We've done something special today mates.

I feel it.

I do.

We've maybe even made some history.

We've sent off a character we fucken love and we've done it with fucken poetry.

See how you love your poems, Jude?

And you love your plays, Dell?

And you love your old fat Italians yelling at the sky, Bert?

Sally, I don't know what you love, but I'm sure there's something?

SALLY: I love this. I love being part of TV.

SHARON: Me too! That's what I was gonna say.

BERT: Marble Bar?

DELL: It's open all night.

SHARON: The way you lot love your wanky arty shit, I love TV.

JUDY: Meet you at the car.

SHARON: I love it. Everything about it. I always have.

I love how we can make things where there was nothing before.

SALLY: Jude, I wrote this spec script. Would you?

SHARON: I love how we can change people's minds about stuff.

JUDY: Of course darling, how exciting!

SHARON: I love how we can make them laugh and cry and take them out of the excrement of their own lives.

In their own living rooms!

Millions of the fuckers at a time! All watching the same thing! All feeling the same feelings!

JUDY: No more deaths, okay? That's the last one I do.

SHARON: And see what we did here today?

BERT: So said Caligula as he slashed the throat of his latest enemy …

JUDY: They're hard.

SHARON: I just have a feeling about it.

I have the feeling that it's important.

That it's the TV version of fucken *Hamlet* or 'I Wandered Lonely as a Cloud' or a Mozart symphony, you know?

JUDY: I haven't written it yet.

SHARON: That people will put this story into their heart and never let it escape.

That when you're eighty years old sipping a piña colada on a cruise to Fiji, Jude, some fellow old fucker will come up to you and throw a drink at you for killing Molly.

In five years' time, ten years' time, twenty years' time, we'll be in at networks pitching new shows and even the receptionist at the front desk while we wait to go in? She'll want to talk about where she was and how heartbroken she was when Molly died.

We've done something fucken spectacular here today, mates.

And you don't know it yet but I do and I feel like the luckiest ex-con in Sydney for it.

There's laughter, maybe another hug?

Righto.

We're all going to meet Jim for a fancy dinner in town now.

Good job.

They leave the story room, turning off the lights as they go.

DUN DUN DUN DUN.

THE END

HOW TO PLOT A HIT IN TWO DAYS

BY MELANIE TAIT

ENSEMBLE THEATRE
DIRECTED BY LEE LEWIS
29 AUGUST 2025 – 11 OCTOBER 2025
WORLD PREMIERE

Ensemble Theatre proudly acknowledges the Cammeraygal people of the Eora Nation as Traditional Custodians of the land on which we stand and share our stories. We pay our respects to Elders past and present.

CAST

AMY INGRAM SHARON
GENEVIEVE LEMON DELL
SEÁN O'SHEA BERT
GEORGIE PARKER JUDY
JULIA ROBERTSON SALLY

CREATIVES

PLAYWRIGHT MELANIE TAIT
DIRECTOR LEE LEWIS
ASSISTANT DIRECTOR TIFFANY WONG
SET & COSTUME DESIGNER SIMONE ROMANIUK
LIGHTING DESIGNER BROCKMAN
COMPOSER & SOUND DESIGNER PAUL CHARLIER
STAGE MANAGER JEN JACKSON
ASSISTANT STAGE MANAGER SHERYDAN SIMSON
COSTUME SUPERVISOR RENATA BESLIK

RUNNING TIME 90 MINUTES NO INTERVAL
REC. AGES 12+
ADULT THEMES, FREQUENT COARSE LANGUAGE

HOW TO PLOT A HIT IN TWO DAYS is a fictional play imagining the machinations of a hypothetical writers' room. It is not affiliated with the television show *A Country Practice*.

This production is made possible by the Commissioners' Circle and The Tracey Trinder Playwright's Award.

Original *A Country Practice* theme composed by Michael Ivan Perjanik, arranged by Paul Charlier.

ABOUT ENSEMBLE THEATRE

Ensemble Theatre is the longest continuously running professional theatre company in Australia and is committed to collaborating with exceptional playwrights and creative talent to present the best international plays, modern classics and new Australian works.

PLAYWRIGHT'S NOTE

A Country Practice was the warm blanket of my childhood.

It wasn't until I was an adult I realised how impactful it was in shaping the things that were important to me: trying to understand my neighbour, living in a community and caring about what I put into the world.

One of the first things I ever wrote, at ten years old, was a script for *A Country Practice* (I believe the storyline involved Luke, Jo, Sarge, Matron and Lucy—Lucy was played by Georgie Parker who I'm absolutely thrilled has brought her considerable talents to the role of Judy). I am a writer, and the kind of writer I am, I believe, because of the hundreds of hours I've spent watching the show.

When my dear friend Kim Lester and I began our podcast *A Country Podcast* in 2020, it was *A Country Practice* writer Judith Colquhoun we wanted to interview more than anyone else – it was the crafting of this incredible show we were more curious about than anything else. How do you create a show that explores social issues, medical problems and a community, without being didactic? How do you keep it fun and propulsive, so it's a pleasure to watch, and not a chore?

What we discovered was a golden age of Australian television: where Australian writers, directors and actors got to fine tune their craft by making two hours of excellent television every week, for most of the year. Creator James Davern's *A Country Practice* was a gift to the audience, and a gift to Australian artists. And a gift with great heart and humour, like the man himself, and the people he brought in to make the show. A subtly morally aspirational show – one that asks us to try and be better people.

I'm grateful Mark Kilmurry thought of me, when he came up with the idea that we needed a play about this remarkable moment in our cultural history – the death of Molly Jones. I'd have been very mad if anyone else dare write it, to be honest, I've spent my whole life preparing for it! And I'm grateful to Lee Lewis for how seriously and open-heartedly she's lept into the world of this theatrical fan fiction!

It's been a pleasure to explore what it is to create at a time when my job, and the jobs of my writer colleagues are constantly being called into question by A-I. This play explores what a group of humans, with human experiences and goals and loves come into a room and create a human hour of television we still talk about forty years later.

I hope this play retains some of the *A Country Practice* DNA — the heart, the humour and the decency. Right now, we're living in a world where those three very important parts of the human experience are being called into question every day.

It's my tribute to Judith Colquhoun, James Davern and the many creative Australians who made a beautiful show that helped teach me how to be a writer and a person.

MELANIE TAIT
PLAYWRIGHT

DIRECTOR'S NOTE

In 1985 the population of Australia was 15.79 million people. On June 5 of that year over half the population, over 8 million people watched the character of Molly Jones die.

In the middle of the decade that included Azaria, Evonne Goolagong, underarm bowling, damming the Franklin, the Sydney Swans, Schindler's Ark, Pavarotti/Sutherland, Ash Wednesday fires, the winged keel, floating the dollar, Medicare, Milperra, the decriminalisation of homosexuality, Uluru returned to the Mutijulu community, Joan Child, the welcome home march for Vietnam veterans, the Fitzgerald Inquiry, the Bicentenary, Kay Cottee and the Newcastle earthquake, the death of a tv character broke the nation's heart. Over two nights, the nation grieved together. For two nights a fiction bound us. A story brought us together. We imagined together.

That story was created by a small group of Australian writers. Those characters were dreamed into existence by Australian creators who lived among us, and wrote stories just for us, because they knew us so well and loved us. In these days of algorithms and the theft of our creators' work by artificial intelligence harvesting machines I see this play as a celebration of the originality, diversity, inventiveness and unique spirit of fully alive writers. I believe that the human brain and the human spirit will always be able to create in a space far beyond any algorithm. Call it the Molly Principle if you like. That night of television could only have been created in the magic space between writer, actor and audience. Wholly human. Deeply moving. Culturally significant.

Sometimes we need reminders of times in our past when we were better humans. I look at the achievements of people and governments of the 1980s and wonder where our compassion went, where we have buried selflessness, when we stopped chaining ourselves to trees for things we believed in. I'm not saying it was a better time – for so many people the racism, the sexism, the homophobia, the parochialism was overwhelming. But I do remember a fight, a vision; leadership towards a better country than the one we accept as Australia in 2025. We were going to be better than this. When I remember, I remember that. And this play makes me remember. Our writers build our memories. They are our national treasures. Thank you to all our writers and of course, to Melanie Tait for reaching across time to the memory of all the *A Country Practice* writers. Mel thank you for your generosity, your humanity and your joy.

And thank you to the whole team at the Ensemble for providing such a gorgeous home for a new Australian play – for your ongoing belief in the importance of our stories.

LEE LEWIS
DIRECTOR

MELANIE TAIT
PLAYWRIGHT

Melanie Tait is a writer for stage and screen with a proven track record in Australia and the UK. Her play THE APPLETON LADIES' POTATO RACE premiered at the Ensemble Theatre in Sydney in March 2019 and toured nationally in 2021. The play has been programmed right around Australia and New Zealand including at the State Theatre Company of South Australia, Queensland Theatre and The Court Theatre in Christchurch. Melanie also adapted the play into a feature film for Paramount+. Her second play for Ensemble, A BROADCAST COUP, opened in January 2023 at Ensemble Theatre as part of Sydney Festival, while THE QUEEN'S NANNY opened in September 2024 at the Ensemble and has just toured Victoria, New South Wales and the ACT. Her first play THE VEGEMITE TALES won critical and popular acclaim, playing eight years in London, including two years on the West End. THE APPLETON LADIES' POTATO RACE, THE QUEEN'S NANNY and HOW TO PLOT A HIT IN TWO DAYS are published by Currency Press and A BROADCAST COUP is published by Playlab. Melanie has an original television series in development with Easy Tiger Productions.

LEE LEWIS
DIRECTOR

Lee Lewis is one of Australia's leading stage directors. She has created over eighty productions around the country. She was the Artistic Director of Griffin Theatre Company and Queensland Theatre. Recent national tours include GASLIGHT and SHIRLEY VALENTINE. For Melbourne Theatre Company she DIRECTED MOTHER PLAY, GLORIA, HAY FEVER and David Williamson's RUPERT which toured to the USA. Selected productions include PRIMA FACIE, THE BLEEDING TREE, FIRST CASUALTY, BERNHARDT/HAMLET (QT) MARY STUART, HONOUR, ZEBRA, LOVE-LIES-BLEEDING, FAMILY VALUES, FIRST LOVE IS THE REVOLUTION, THE ALMIGHTY SOMETIMES, KILL CLIMATE DENIERS, THE HOMOSEXUALS OR 'FAGGOTS', MASQUERADE, EMERALD CITY, A RABBIT FOR KIM JONG IL, SILENT DISCO, RETURN TO THE DIRT, A SMURF IN WANDERLAND, THE BULL THE MOON AND THE CORONET OF STARS, THE NIGHTWATCHMAN, THE LITERATI, THAT FACE, TINY BEAUTIFUL THINGS, A NUMBER, THIS HEAVEN, HALF AND HALF, THE CALL and TWELFTH NIGHT. She holds two masters in theatre, has won Helpmann, Green Room, Sydney Theatre Awards and Glugs for her work. In 2024 she was awarded an OAM for services to Australian playwriting. She loves her job.

TIFFANY WONG
ASSISTANT DIRECTOR

Assistant Director, Ensemble Theatre: EMERALD CITY. Sydney Theatre Company: TOP COAT. Associate Director, Bell Shakespeare: KING LEAR. Directorial Assistant: Hayes Theatre Co: MURDER FOR TWO. Director, New Theatre: ATLANTIS. Slanted Theatre: BOOM, SHORT BLANKET, LADY PRECIOUS STREAM, THREE FAT VIRGINS UNASSEMBLED, CHING CHONG CHINAMAN. Actor, Australian Shakespeare Company: ROMEO AND JULIET. Joining The Dots: THE MAGICIAN'S NEPHEW. Your Side: TWO WORLDS, ONE HEART. Film: FIVE BLIND DATES. Audition Coordinator/ Stage Manager, Crossroads Live: CATS, BACK TO THE FUTURE, HAIRSPRAY, TEG. Dainty: TINA – THE TINA TURNER MUSICAL. Awards: Tiffany was featured as an Honouree of the Asian Australian

2022, 2023 & 2024 List and is a proud member of Actors Equity.

AMY INGRAM

SHARON

Ensemble Theatre Debut. The Good Room: I SHOULD HAVE DRUNK MORE CHAMPAGNE, I WANT TO KNOW WHAT LOVE IS (INC NATIONAL TOUR), I JUST CAME TO SAY GOODBYE, ONE BOTTLE LATER. Elbow Room: WE GET IT. Justin Martin and Old Fitz: LOW LEVEL PANIC. La Boite Theatre: COSI, THE TRAGEDY OF KING RICHARD THE THIRD, BLACKROCK. MML Worldwide: MAGIC MIKE LIVE AUSTRALIAN TOUR. Metro Arts Awkward Conversations: MEDEA REDUX. Myths Made Here: CINDERELLA. Queensland Theatre: FAT PIG, SEEDING BED, TROLLOP, THE SEAGULL, THE ODD COUPLE, BERNHARDT HAMLET, FAMILY VALUES, PRIDE AND PREJUDICE. Shake & Stir: OUT DAMN SNOT, FOURTEEN (INC NATIONAL TOUR). Woodward and Neil Golding Productions: THE COMPLETE WORKS OF WILLIAM SHAKESPEARE ABRIDGED. Film: DEMON DISORDER, POSTHUMOUS. Television/Media: INA, APPLES NEVER FALL, BOY SWALLOWS UNIVERSE, IN OUR BLOOD, JOE VS CAROL, YOUNG ROCK and 2 YEARS LATER.

GENEVIEVE LEMON

DELL

Ensemble Theatre: FOLK, DIPLOMACY, WHO'S AFRAID OF VIRGINIA WOOLF, TRIBES, BROKEN GLASS. Belvoir Street Theatre: DEATH OF A SALESMAN, SEVENTEEN. Griffin Theatre Company: THE HOMOSEXUALS OR THE 'FAGGOTS'. Hayes Theatre Company: DUBBO CHAMPIONSHIP

WRESTLING, VIOLET, MELBA, CAROLINE OR CHANGE. Sydney Theatre Company: BRILLIANT LIES, THE HANGING, THE GIRL WHO SAW EVERYTHING, HANGING MAN, HARBOUR, MERRILY WE ROLL ALONG, MIRACLE CITY, MORNING SACRIFICE, NOISES OFF, ONCE IN A LIFETIME, THE RECRUIT, THE REPUBLIC OF MYOPIA, SUMMER RAIN, VICTORY. Other Theatre Credits: SISTER ACT, BILLY ELLIOT: THE MUSICAL, PRISCILLA QUEEN OF THE DESERT: THE MUSICAL, THE PIRATES OF PENZANCE, THE MOUSETRAP. Film: SWEETIE, THE PIANO, THE POWER OF THE DOG, TICKET TO PARADISE, HERE OUT WEST, ACUTE MISFORTUNE, THE DRESSMAKER, BILLY'S HOLIDAY, HOLY SMOKE, SOFT FRUIT, SURBURBAN MAYHEM, LADIES IN BLACK, THE APPLETON LADIES' POTATO RACE, CRUEL HANDS, RUNT, KANGAROO. Television: RETURN TO PARADISE, POPULATION 11, PIECES OF HER, COLIN FROM ACCOUNTS, THE TOURIST, EDEN, FRAYED, THREE MEN AND A BABY GRAND, TOP OF THE LAKE, PRISONER. Awards: Helpmann Award, Green Room Awards, Sydney Theatre Critic's Award, Australian Film Critic's Award.

SEÁN O'SHEA

BERT

Ensemble Theatre: NEARER THE GODS, THE RASPUTIN AFFAIR, TRIBES, THE CAVALCADERS, SWEET ROAD. Other Theatre: Sydney Theatre Company: THE SEAGULL, THE IMPORTANCE OF BEING EARNEST, SAINT JOAN, DINNER, A FLEA IN HER EAR, MARIAGE BLANC, THE CRUCIBLE, SCENES FROM A SEPARATION, THE WAY OF THE WORLD. Melbourne Theatre Company: RUPERT. Red Line Productions: AMADEUS. Belvoir: TELL ME I'M HERE. Bell Shakespeare: THE MISER, HAMLET, TARTUFFE, HENRY IV, THE DUCHESS OF MALFI, MUCH ADO ABOUT NOTHING, MEASURE FOR MEASURE, THE COMEDY OF ERRORS, MACBETH.

STCSA: THE TAMING OF THE SHREW. Griffin Theatre: WOLF LULLABY. Western Australian Theatre Company: THE CHERRY ORCHARD, WOMAN IN MIND. Sport For Jove: THE PLAYER KINGS. Australian Ballet: OSCAR. Training: Western Australian Academy of Performing Arts.

GEORGIE PARKER
JUDY

Ensemble Theatre: THE GREAT DIVIDE, RHINESTONE REX AND MISS MONICA (Revival), MURDER ON THE WIRELESS, LUNA GALE, BAREFOOT IN THE PARK, RAPTURE BLISTER BURN, LET THE SUNSHINE, RABBIT HOLE, THEY'RE PLAYING OUR SONG, CHAPTER TWO. Footbridge Theatre and National tour: HOW TO SUCCEED IN BUSINESS WITHOUT REALLY TRYING. NUNSENSE. Marion St Theatre: WAIT UNTIL DARK, HERE COMES SHOWTIME. Melbourne Theatre Company: HIGH SOCIETY. Queensland Theatre: RHINESTONE REX AND MISS MONICA, THREEPENNY OPERA. Sydney Theatre Company: SCENES FROM A SEPARATION, ALL IN THE TIMING. Theatre Royal: CRAZY FOR YOU. Tilbury Hotel: GRIN AND BERRET. Sydney Entertainment Centre and National tour: MAN FROM SNOWY RIVER. FILM: THE 13TH SUMMER, THE STRANGER (short film) SANTA'S APPRENTICE (animation), IRRESISTIBLE, DANGER DOWN UNDER, YOUNG EINSTEIN, THE REPRISAL, THE BOY WHO HAD EVERYTHING, THE 13TH FLOOR. Television: HOME AND AWAY, PLAY SCHOOL, CITY HOMICIDE, SCORCHED, EMERALD FALLS, STUPID STUPID MAN, STEPFATHER OF THE BRIDE, THE SOCIETY MURDERS, ALL SAINTS, FIRE, OVER THE HILL, ACROPOLIS NOW, GP, ALL TOGETHER NOW, A COUNTRY PRACTICE, RAFFERTY'S RULES, BARLOW AND CHAMBERS, WILLING and ABEL.

Georgie has been nominated for a Logie Award 11 times and won 7, two of them Gold for her television work.

JULIA ROBERTSON
SALLY

Actor; Ensemble Theatre Debut. Belvoir 25A: POV (with re:group), JESS AND JOE FOREVER (with Sugary Rum Productions), THE ASTRAL PLANE. Christine Dunstan Productions: TIM. Griffin Theatre Company: WHEREVER SHE WANDERS. Little Eggs Collective: THE LOST BOYS. Sydney Theatre Company: THE REAL THING. Film: HOT MESS. As Director; Little Eggs Collective: PINOCCHIO, THE RIME OF THE ANCIENT MARINER, EXTENDED PLAY: OLIVER SHERMACHER (with City Recital Hall), METROPOLIS (with Hayes Theatre Co.) Joshua Robson Productions: THE PRODUCERS (with Hayes Theatre Co & Riverside Parramatta). RaCreate & Old Fitz Theatre: DO YOU MIND? Assistant Director; Ensemble Theatre: THE GREAT DIVIDE, THE HEARTBREAK CHOIR. Joshua Robson Productions & Hayes Theatre Co: BONNIE AND CLYDE, CITY OF ANGELS. Opera Australia: IL TRITTICO. Training: Lee Strasberg Institute of Theatre and Film (New York) and the Royal Academy of Dramatic Art (London).

SIMONE ROMANIUK
SET AND COSTUME DESIGNER

Ensemble Theatre: THE LOVER & THE DUMB WAITER, SUDDENLY LAST SUMMER, CLYDE'S, HONOUR, KENNY, THE LAST WIFE, LUNA GALE, SHIRLEY VALENTINE, FRANKENSTEIN, CASANOVA. Brisbane Festival: BANANALAND (with Sydney Festival), MACBETH. Queensland Theatre: TINY BEAUTIFUL THINGS (with Belvoir),

THE ALMIGHTY SOMETIMES, BERNHARDT/HAMLET, MACBETH, ELIZABETH: ALMOST BY CHANCE A WOMAN, VENUS IN FUR, BOMBSHELLS, KELLY, HEAD FULL OF LOVE, FRACTIONS, THE LITTLE DOG LAUGHED, AUSTRALIA DAY, THE PITCH, THE CHINA INCIDENT, THE REMOVALISTS, AN OAK TREE, MAN EQUALS MAN, WAITING FOR GODOT, EATING ICE CREAM, BECKETT X 3, RUBY MOON. Sydney Theatre Company: THE CRUCIBLE, SENECA'S THYESTES. Opera Queensland: THE MIKADO, THE MERRY WIDOW, SPACE ENCOUNTERS, THE MAGIC FLUTE. Pinchgut Opera: RINALDO. State Opera South Australia: LA BOHEME, SUMMER OF THE SEVENTEENTH DOLL, LOVE BURNS, BOOJUM!. Victorian Opera: EUCALYPTUS.

BROCKMAN
LIGHTING DESIGNER

Ensemble Theatre: TRIBES, THE BIG DRY, THE PLANT, NEVILLE'S ISLAND. Campbelltown Arts Centre: HIGH OCTANE, MIRAGE; Dance Makers Collective: ALL IN, THE RIVOLI, WOLVERINE. Darlinghurst Theatre Company: OVERFLOW, TORCH SONG TRILOGY, BROKEN. Griffin Theatre Company: FLAT EARTHERS, FAMILY VALUES, SPLINTER, REPLAY, DIVING FOR PEARLS. Hayes Theatre Company: RIDE THE CYCLONE, GENTLEMEN PREFER BLONDES, CARMEN ALIVE OR DEAD, RAZORHURST. National Theatre of Paramatta: THINGS HIDDEN SINCE THE FOUNDATION OF THE WORLD (AUS/UK), LADY TABOULI, GIRL IN THE MACHINE, THE GIRL/THE WOMAN, THE SORRY MUM PROJECT, LET ME KNOW WHEN YOU GET HOME. Queensland Theatre Company: FAMILY VALUES. Sydney Theatre Company: CIRCLE MIRROR TRANSFORMATION, CONSTELLATIONS,

AMERICAN SIGNS, A FOOL IN LOVE. Awards: APDG Award for best lighting design for a Live Performance or Event (CLEANSED), Best Lighting Design for an Mainstage Production 2023 (CONSTELLATIONS), Best Lighting Design for an Independent Production 2019 (METAMORPHOSES), Best Lighting Design for an Independent Production 2021 (SYMPHONIE FANTASTIQUE).

PAUL CHARLIER
COMPOSER AND SOUND DESIGNER

Belvoir Street Theatre: FAITH HEALER, DANCE OF DEATH, BURIED CHILD, DIARY OF A MAD MAN, AFTERSHOCKS, HAMLET, THE BLIND GIANT IS DANCING, SUDDENLY LAST SUMMER, THE LIEUTENANT OF INISHMORE. Broadway: DEUCE. Crossroads Live: AND THEN THERE WERE NONE. DV8 Physical Theatre: THE COST OF LIVING. Force Majeure: ALREADY ELSEWHERE. Griffin Theatre Company: PRIMA FACIE. Legs on the Wall & Sydney Opera House: HONOUR BOUND. Marrugeku: JURRUNGU NGAN-GA (STRAIGHT TALK). National Theatre of Great Britain: AFTERLIFE. NewTheatricals: GASLIGHT. Sydney Theatre Company: RBG-OF MANY ONE, A STREETCAR NAMED DESIRE, UNCLE VANYA, TOT MOM, COPENHAGEN. Film: CANDY, LAST RIDE, LOOKING FOR ALIBRANDI, PAUL KELLY STORIES OF ME, ADAM GOODES THE FINAL QUARTER, SUZY AND THE SIMPLE MAN, RACHEL'S FARM, HOLDING THE MAN, THE PROJECTIONIST, THE COST OF LIVING, THE POOL. Television: AFTERSHOCKS. Awards: Helpmann Award, Sydney Theatre Awards and Australian Screen Sound Guild Award.

JEN JACKSON
STAGE MANAGER

Stage Manager: Ensemble Theatre: MASTER CLASS. Belvoir Street Theatre: LOSE TO WIN. Carriageworks: PARTY | PROTEST | REMEMBER. Contemporary Asian Australian Performance: LOST IN SHANGHAI, THE BRIDAL LAMENT, DOUBLE DELICIOUS. Griffin Theatre Company: KOREABOO, GOLDEN BLOOD 黄金血液, PONY, END OF. Kurinji & Sydney Festival: 宿 (STAY). National Theatre of Parramatta: NOTHING. The Ethics Centre: FESTIVAL OF DANGEROUS IDEAS 2022. Assistant Stage Manager: Belvoir St Theatre: SONG OF FIRST DESIRE, AT WHAT COST. Pinchgut Opera: RINALDO. Company Manager: National Theatre of Parramatta: CHOIR BOY. Training: NATIONAL INSTITUTE OF DRAMATIC ART.

SHERYDAN SIMSON
ASSISTANT STAGE MANAGER

Ensemble Theatre: Stage Manager Cover: PRIMARY TRUST, THE LOVER AND THE DUMB WAITER. Stage Manager for Steps and Holes: A PILGRIM IN SEARCH FOR A BULL NAMED CARLO. Bub Productions in association with 25a: HOT TUB. Hayes Theatre Company: PIRATES OF PENZANCE (or the Slave of Duty). Sydney Conservatorium of Music: PAPER STARS. Production manager for Griffin Theatre Company: KOREABOO. Joshua Robson Productions in association with Hayes Theatre Company: LITTLE WOMEN. The Other Theatre Company: IRL. Site assistant for City of Sydney: NEW YEARS EVE 2025 and NEW YEARS

EVE 2024. Access and inclusion assistant for City of Sydney: SYDNEY CHRISTMAS CONCERTS 2024. Training: National Institute of Dramatic Art: Production; Bachelor of Fine Arts (Technical Theatre and Stage Management). University of New England: Diploma of Arts.

RENATA BESLIK
COSTUME SUPERVISOR

Ensemble Theatre: EMERALD CITY, ARIA, UNCLE VANYA, MASTER CLASS, ULSTER AMERICAN, SWITZERLAND, ALONE IT STANDS, THE GREAT DIVIDE, THE MEMORY OF WATER, SUMMER OF HAROLD, MR BAILEY'S MINDER, BENEFACTORS, RHINESTONE REX AND MISS MONICA, THE CARETAKER, PHOTOGRAPH 51, THE ONE, OUTDATED, CRUNCH TIME, BABY DOLL, FOLK, LUNA GALE, and many more. Bell Shakespeare: HENRY V, THE WINTER'S TALE, MACBETH. Belvoir St Theatre: FANGIRLS. New Theatricals: DARKNESS. National Institute of Dramatic Art: THE GOVERNMENT INSPECTOR, STAY HAPPY KEEP SMILING, THE TEMPEST, WOYCECK, A LIE OF THE MIND, PORT, THE THREESOME. Pinchgut Opera: THE FAIRY QUEEN, JULIUS CAESAR, RINALDO, MÉDÉE, PLATÉE and many more. Sydney Festival: BETTY BLOKKBUSTER RE-IMAGINED. Australian Chamber Orchestra: THE NUTCRACKER.

SUPPORT US

Every dollar counts. Ensemble relies on self-earned income to deliver all the programs that we do – commissioning new work, education outreach, producing world premieres, so please think about your capacity to make a gift to Ensemble. You can donate online at ensemble.com.au/support-us or contact Stephen Attfield, Philanthropy & Partnerships Manager, on **stephena@ensemble.com.au** or via **02 8918 3400.**

LIFE PATRONS

Those who have made significant contributions to Ensemble:

The Balnaves Foundation
Clitheroe Foundation
Jinnie & Ross Gavin
Ingrid Kaiser
Graham McConnochie
Neilson Foundation
Jenny Reynolds & Guy Reynolds AO
George & Diana Shirling
Southern Steel Group Pty Ltd

PLATINUM $20,000+

The Balnaves Foundation
Giving Support Foundation
Graham Bradley AM & Charlene Bradley
Clitheroe Foundation
Ingrid Kaiser
McConnochie Family Fund
Neilson Foundation
Jenny Reynolds & Guy Reynolds AO
Hon. Warwick Smith AO & Kathryn Smith
Southern Steel Group Pty Ltd
Christine Thomson
Anonymous x 1

GOLD $10,000+

Diane Balnaves
The Boleyn Foundation
Darin Cooper Foundation
Peter Eichhorn & Anne Willems
APS Foundation - Brent & Vicki Emmett Giving Fund
Alan Gunn & Kerri Fogg
Debbie, Garry & Val
Jinnie & Ross Gavin
In Memory of John Power
John & Diana Smythe Foundation
Philip Maxwell & Jane Tham
Annie & Graham Williams
Anonymous

SILVER $5,000+

David Z Burger Foundation
Wayne Cahill
The Giving Fund & Sally Collier
Emma Hodgman & John Coorey
Prue & Andrew Kennard
David Pumphrey OAM & Jill Pumphrey
Anonymous

BRONZE $1,000+

Margaret Andrews
Paul Bedbrook & Fiona Hopkins
Ellen Borda
Anne Bruning
Alison Carmine
Lynette Casey & Patricia Zancanaro
Margaret Cassidy
Anne Clark
Debby Cramer
Valerie Crawford
Ralph Davis
Laurence Dillon
Nancy Fox AM & Bruce Arnold
Friends of Tracey Trinder
Bruce & Jo Hambrett
Andrew & Wendy Hamlin
Richard Hansford
Matilda Hartwell
Yvonne Hazell OAM
The Hilmer Family Endowment
Carolyn Hum
Jacqueline Katz
John Lewis
Peter Lowry AM & Dr Carolyn Lowry OAM
Helen Markiewicz
Catriona Morgan-Hunn
Peter EJ Murray
Barbara Osborne
Jim & Maggie Pritchitt
Dorelle & Bruce Propert
Angus & Elspeth Richards
Monica & Gary Robinson
Megan & Tim Sjoquist
Holly Stein
Bob Taffel
Neil Tait
Geoffrey Tebbutt
Judy Thomson
Lynn Trainor
Wendy Trevor Jones
Gai & Tony Wales
Geoffrey & Helen Webber
Dr Eric Wegman
Julia Wokes
Anonymous x 4

COMMISSIONERS' CIRCLE

Supporting new Australian work

Diane Balnaves
Graham Bradley AM & Charlene Bradley
Paul Clitheroe AM & Vicki Clitheroe
Jennifer Darin & Dennis Cooper
Alan Gunn & Kerri Fogg
Ingrid Kaiser
Steve & Julie Murphy
Alicia Powell
Jenny Reynolds & Guy Reynolds AO
George & Diana Shirling
Jane Tham & Philip Maxwell
Christine Thomson

LEAVE A LEGACY

We would like to thank the following Estates for their generous donations

Estate of the late Freddie Bluhm
Estate of the late Jayati Dutta
Estate of the late Jennifer Fulton
Estate of the late Helen Gordon
Estate of the late Leo Mamontoff
Estates of the late Zika & Dimitry Nesteroff
Estate of the late Margaret Stenhouse

ENCORE CIRCLE

Thank you to the following people for bequests in their wills:

Liz Barton
Valerie Crawford
Mark Midwinter
Joe Sbarro
Junia Vaz de Melo
Anonymous x 6

Supporters are recognized for 12 months from the date of donation. Current at 15 July 2024.

OUR PARTNERS

Thank you to our partners for playing a vital role in our success.

MAJOR PARTNER

ASSOCIATE PARTNER

STRATEGIC PARTNER

SUPPORTING PARTNERS

ENSEMBLE ED PARTNERS

ENSEMBLE HOSPITALITY PARTNERS

ENSEMBLE THEATRE TEAM

Artistic Director **Mark Kilmurry**
Executive Director **Loretta Busby**
Chief Financial Officer **David Balfour Wright**
Senior Producer **Carly Pickard**
Associate Producer **Saint Clair**
Literary Manager **Sarah Odillo Maher**
Production Manager **Paisley Williams**
Technical Manager **Gayda de Mesa**
Resident Stage Manager **Lauren Tulloh**
Philanthropy and Partnerships Manager **Stephen Attfield**
Marketing Manager **Rachael McDonnell**
Deputy Marketing Manager **Charlotte Burgess**
Education and Community Coordinator **Sophie Kelly**
Marketing Assistant **Emma Garden**
Media Relations **Kabuku PR**
Administrative Support **Jordan Gillett**
In-house Designer **Cheryl Ward**
Ticketing Services Manager **Spiros Hristias**
Ticketing Customer Service and Office Coordinator **Aimee Timmins**
Box Office Team **Mary Barakate, Kyra Belford-Thomas, Allan Lyra Chang, Angus Evans, Alishia Keane, Marina McCaul & Kathryn Siely**
Finance Assistant **Gita Sugiyanto**
Front of House Manager **Jim Birch**
Front of House Supervisors **Megan Cribb, Jaro Murany, Ben Sullivan & Bella Wellstead**
Head Chef **Ian Paul Aguilar Alarcon**
Restaurant Manager **Amy Mitchell**
Building Manager **Paul Craig**

ENSEMBLE LIMITED BOARD

Chair Graham Bradley AM, John Bayley, Narelle Beattie, Mark Kilmurry, Anne-Marie McGinty, James Sherrard & Trent Zimmerman

ENSEMBLE FOUNDATION BOARD

Chair Paul Clitheroe AM, Diane Balnaves, Graham Bradley AM, Alison Cameron, Joanne Cunningham, Ross Gavin, Mark Kilmurry & David Pumphrey OAM

ENSEMBLE AMBASSADORS

Todd McKenney, Brian Meegan, Georgie Parker & Kate Raison